my **revis**

BIRMINGHAM METROPOLITAN COLLEGE

273951

ID0245733

AS Edexcel History
PURSUING LIFE AND LIBERTY:
EQUALITY IN THE USA
1945–68

Robin Bunce and
Laura Gallagher

HODDER
EDUCATION
AN HACHETTE UK COMPANY

SUTTON COLDFIELD CAMPUS

Birmingham
Metropolitan
College LRC

Accession	
273951	
Class	
Date Catalogued	

Hachette UK's policy is to use papers that are natural, renewable and recyclable products and made from wood grown in sustainable forests. The logging and manufacturing processes are expected to conform to the environmental regulations of the country of origin.

Orders: please contact Bookpoint Ltd, 130 Milton Park, Abingdon, Oxon OX14 4SB. Telephone: +44 (0)1235 827720. Fax: +44 (0)1235 400454. Lines are open 9.00a.m.–5.00p.m., Monday to Saturday, with a 24-hour message answering service. Visit our website at www.hoddereducation. co.uk.

© Robin Bunce and Laura Gallagher 2011
First published in 2011 by
Hodder Education,
an Hachette UK company
338 Euston Road
London NW1 3BH

Impression number   10 9 8 7 6 5 4 3 2 1
Year   2015 2014 2013 2012 2011

All rights reserved. Apart from any use permitted under UK copyright law, no part of this publication may be reproduced or transmitted in any form or by any means, electronic or mechanical, including photocopying and recording, or held within any information storage and retrieval system, without permission in writing from the publisher or under licence from the Copyright Licensing Agency Limited. Further details of such licences (for reprographic reproduction) may be obtained from the Copyright Licensing Agency Limited, Saffron House, 6–10 Kirby Street, London EC1N 8TS.

Cover photo © Photodisc/Getty Images
Typeset in 11/13 Stempel Schneidler by Pantek Media
Artwork by Pantek Media
Printed and bound in India

A catalogue record for this title is available from the British Library

ISBN 978 1 444 152 135

Contents

Introduction

About Unit 1

Unit 1 is worth 50 per cent of your AS level. It requires detailed knowledge of a historical period and the ability to explain the causes, consequences and significance of historical events. There are no sources in the Unit 1 exam and therefore all marks available are awarded for use of your own knowledge.

In the exam, you are required to answer two questions from a range of options. The questions are all worth 30 marks and therefore you should divide your time – including any extra time you have been allocated – equally between the questions.

The questions you answer must be on different topics. This book deals exclusively with topic D5: Pursuing Life and Liberty: Equality in the USA, 1945–68. However, you must also be prepared to answer a question on another topic.

The exam will test your ability to:

- select information that focuses on the question
- organise this information to provide an answer to the question
- show range and depth in the examples you provide
- analyse the significance of the information used to reach an overall judgement.

Pursuing Life and Liberty: Equality in the USA, 1945–68

The exam board specifies that students should study four general areas as part of this topic.

1. The social and economic position of black citizens in the USA, 1945–55.
2. Martin Luther King and peaceful protest, 1955–68.
3. Black Power and the use of violence.
4. The changing economic and social environment of the 1960s.

How to use this book

This book has been designed to help you to develop the knowledge and skills necessary to succeed in the exam. The book is divided into four sections – one for each general area of the course. Each section is made up of a series of topics organised into double-page spreads. On the left-hand page, you will find a summary of the key content you need to learn. Words in bold in the key content are defined in the glossary (see pages 62–65). On the right-hand page, you will find exam-focused activities. Together, these two strands of the book will take you through the knowledge and skills essential for exam success.

▼ Key historical content

▼ Exam-focused activities

There are three levels of exam-focused activities.

- Band 1 activities are designed to develop the foundational skills needed to pass the exam. These have a turquoise heading and this symbol:

- Band 2 activities are designed to build on the skills developed in Band 1 activities and to help you achieve a C grade. These have an orange heading and this symbol:

- Band 3 activities are designed to enable you to access the highest grades. These have a purple heading and this symbol:

Some of the activities have answers or suggested answers on pages 66–69 and have the following symbol to indicate this: (a)

Others are intended for you to complete in pairs and assess by comparing answers. These do not have answers.

Each section ends with an exam-style question, and a model A-grade answer with examiner's commentary. This should give you guidance on what is required to achieve the top grades.

You can also keep track of your revision by ticking off each topic heading in the book, or by ticking the checklist on the contents page. Tick each box when you have:

- revised and understood a topic
- completed the activities.

Mark scheme

For some of the activities in this book, it will be useful to refer to the mark scheme for the unit. Below is the mark scheme for Unit 1.

Level	Marks	Description
1	1–6	• Lacks focus on the question. • Limited factual accuracy. • Highly generalised. *Level 1 answers are highly simplistic, irrelevant or vague.*
2	7–12	• General points with some focus on the question. • Some accurate and relevant supporting evidence. *Level 2 answers might tell the story without addressing the question, or address the question without providing supporting examples.*
3	13–18	• General points that focus on the question. • Accurate support, but this may be either only partly relevant or lacking detail, or both. • Attempted analysis. *Level 3 answers attempt to focus on the question, but have significant areas of weakness. For example, the focus on the question may drift, the answer may lack specific examples, or parts of the essay may simply tell the story. Answers that do not deal with factors that are stated in the question cannot achieve higher than Level 3.*
4	19–24	• General points that clearly focus on the question and show understanding of the most important factors involved. • Accurate, relevant and detailed supporting evidence. • Analysis. *Level 4 answers clearly attempt to answer the question and demonstrate a detailed and wide-ranging knowledge of the period studied.*
5	25–30	• As Level 4 • Sustained analysis. *Level 5 answers are thorough and detailed. They clearly engage with the question and offer a balanced and carefully reasoned argument, which is sustained throughout the essay.*

Section 1: The social and economic position of black citizens in the USA, 1945–55

The position of black Americans in 1945

Revised

The origins of segregation

By the nineteenth century, around 12 million Africans had been brought to America as **slaves**. Following the **American Civil War** of 1861–65, slavery was abolished. **Constitutional Amendments** were added to the American **Constitution** to guarantee the rights of former slaves.

- Fourteenth Amendment – gave equal citizenship rights to everyone born in America.
- Fifteenth Amendment – gave voting rights to all citizens regardless of race.

Segregation

In spite of **emancipation**, black Americans were still not free. From the 1890s onwards, many **Southern states** introduced **racial segregation** in the form of **Jim Crow laws**.

Plessy v. Ferguson

In 1896 a black man, Homer Plessy, challenged segregation laws, claiming that they were incompatible with the Fourteenth Amendment. The **Supreme Court** ruled that segregation was legal because it was legitimate to treat people according to the principle 'separate but equal'.

North and South before the Second World War

The condition of black Americans varied in different parts of America.

- In the Southern states, legal segregation was widespread. Also, the vast majority of black Americans were **disenfranchised** by **grandfather clauses** and **literacy tests**. Finally, the Ku Klux Klan (**KKK**) terrorised black Americans using techniques such as **lynching**.
- By contrast, in the **Northern states**, segregation was rare. What is more, Black Americans had greater access to higher-paid industrial jobs and many were organised in unions. However, on average, black workers earned 50 per cent less than their white counterparts. Many black people could vote. Black Americans tended to live in **ghettos**.

The Second World War and race relations

The Second World War had a threefold impact on race relations.

There was an obvious contradiction between fighting **Nazi** racism in Europe and allowing racism to go unchallenged in America. Black soldiers adopted the **Double V** sign, symbolising that they were fighting for a victory against racism in Europe and America.

Black soldiers spent much of the war in Britain, where there was no segregation. Moreover, in America, around 500,000 black Americans migrated North to work in war-related industrial jobs. Consequently, many black Americans experienced more integrated societies.

Black people who had fought for their country during the war expected better treatment on their return. Furthermore, black heroes, such as the American airman **Woodrow Crockett**, won the respect of white soldiers due to their outstanding courage.

The impact of the Second World War

The Second World War affected political and economic rights for black Americans.

Southern states

- In 1945, **civil rights groups** ran **voter registration campaigns**. The proportion of black voters rose from two per cent in 1940 to fifteen per cent in 1945.
- Unemployment among black Americans fell from 900,000 in 1940 to 150,000 in 1945.

Northern states

- Migration caused the proportion of black people in the North to rise dramatically. In sixteen states, the black population was more than five per cent and therefore had significant voting power.
- Between 1943–1945, two black **Congressmen** were elected to serve in Northern states.

❗ Complete the paragraph

Below are a sample exam-style question and a paragraph written in answer to this question. The paragraph contains a point and specific examples, but lacks a concluding explanatory link back to the question. Complete the paragraph adding this link in the space provided.

How far was the Second World War the main reason for advancements in black civil rights in the period 1945–55?

The Second World War was an important reason for the advancement in black civil rights in the period 1945–55. For example, the Second World War led to the mass migration of black workers from the Southern states to the North. Around half a million black Americans made this journey and received higher wages in Northern industry as a result. Equally, the Second World War highlighted the evil of racism in Europe. Black soldiers who fought against Nazi racism started making the Double V sign to show that they were fighting against racism at home as well as abroad. Finally, black airmen, such as Woodrow Crockett, were regarded as heroes by white officers and white soldiers.

_____

_____

❙ Identify an argument

Below are a series of definitions, a sample exam-style question and two sample conclusions. One of the conclusions achieves a high level because it contains an argument. The other achieves a lower level because it contains only description and assertion. Identify which is which. The mark scheme on page 3 will help you.

- **Description:** a detailed account.
- **Assertion:** a statement of fact or an opinion that is not supported by a reason.
- **Reason:** a statement that explains or justifies something.
- **Argument:** an assertion justified with a reason.

How significant was the Second World War in the achievement of black civil rights in the period 1945–55?

Sample 1

The Second World War was significant for advancing black civil rights in several ways. Following the war, more black voters registered to vote. Additionally, black people were elected to the American Congress. Finally, the experience of life in Europe persuaded many black soldiers that integration could be successful. Therefore, the Second World War was very important in achieving civil rights for black people.

Sample 2

The Second World War was significant in the achievement of black civil rights because it led to an improvement in the status of black people. However, the impact of the Second World War was limited in the sense that it did nothing to address racial segregation or its legal foundation – Plessy v. Ferguson. On the one hand, black soldiers returned as heroes and black workers who moved to the North were paid better, and therefore in both senses the status of black people improved. On the other hand, black soldiers returned to a country where segregation was still considered legal across the South. Therefore, while the Second World War was important in improving the status of black people, there were still significant problems that were not addressed.

President Truman and civil rights

Revised

Harry S. Truman (President 1945–53)

Traditionally, black Americans had voted for the **Republican Party**. President Truman was able to win considerable black support for the **Democratic Party** by endorsing civil rights during his presidency. Truman was motivated by his experience of segregation in his home state of Missouri, by the heroism of black war veterans, and by the **Cold War**.

The impact of the Cold War

The injustice of segregation undermined America's claim to be fighting for 'freedom and justice' in the Cold War. Consequently, Truman knew that he had to address racism as part of his campaign to win the Cold War.

'To Secure These Rights', 1947

Truman established the President's Committee on Civil Rights to investigate racism in America. Its report, entitled 'To Secure These Rights', highlighted inequalities and made suggestions for change.

Inequalities	Suggestions for change
• Lynching was widespread in the Southern states. • The police used barbaric methods, including **pistol-whipping**, against black prisoners. • Legal obstacles prevented many black Americans from voting. • White workers received, on average, 20 cents per hour more than black workers. • In 1940, there was one doctor for every 3,300 black patients. In contrast, there was one doctor for every 750 white patients.	• Anti-lynching laws. • New powers for the **Federal Government** to enforce civil rights. • Government contracts should not be given to racist employers. • New laws to curb police brutality. • All obstacles to voting should be outlawed. • A Civil Rights Act to outlaw segregation in education and healthcare.

Other actions

Truman used his powers as president to implement the following reforms.

Employment

- **Executive order** 9980 (1948) outlawed racial discrimination in **civil service** employment.
- The Committee on Government Contract Compliance (CGCC) was established in 1951 to ensure that government contracts did not go to racist employers.
- Truman appointed a number of black Americans to high-profile government jobs. For example, he made Ralph Bunche Ambassador to the **United Nations**.

Desegregation

- Executive order 9981 (1948) ended segregation in the army.
- Truman's **inauguration** ceremony in 1949 was desegregated.
- In 1950, the canteen at Washington Airport was desegregated. Truman was aware that foreign dignitaries arrived at Washington Airport. He did not want their first experience of America to include segregation.

Housing

- The **Fair Deal** programme committed the Government to building large numbers of new homes, particularly in inner-city ghettos.

The impact of Truman's measures

Truman failed to implement many of the recommendations in 'To Secure These Rights'. He did not pass anti-lynching laws and he did not address segregation in education and healthcare. Moreover, some of his measures failed to achieve great change. The Fair Deal housing programme was underfunded and therefore demolished more houses than it actually built. Nonetheless, 'To Secure These Rights' was a turning point in race relations because it showed that the Federal Government had recognised its responsibility to address racism in America.

Spot the mistake
ⓐ

Below are a sample exam-style question and a paragraph written in answer to this question. Why does this paragraph not get into Level 4? Once you have identified the mistake, rewrite the paragraph so that it displays the qualities of Level 4. The mark scheme on page 3 will help you.

How successful was the Federal Government in tackling racial inequality in the period 1945–53?

The Federal Government made some progress in tackling racial inequality in the period 1945–53. For example, the President was concerned that black people were not being treated fairly in America, even though he had been born in a state where segregation was a fact of life. Therefore, he commissioned a report to make recommendations about what to do about the problems of racial inequality in America. The report said a series of things were wrong in America and that the Government should take action to ensure that black people were not subject to racial discrimination. In this way, the Government made some progress in tackling racial inequality because, for the first time, the President made it Government business to address discrimination.

Turning assertion into argument
ⓐ

Below are a sample exam-style question and a series of assertions. Read the exam-style question and then add a justification to each of the assertions to turn it into an argument.

How successful was the Federal Government in tackling racial inequality in the period 1945–53?

President Truman's attempts to desegregate public places did little to tackle racial inequality in the sense that
_____
_____

'To Secure These Rights' had a limited impact on racial inequality in the sense that
_____
_____

President Truman's employment reforms had a moderate impact on racial inequality in the sense that
_____
_____

Early campaigns

Following the Second World War, there was increasing **grass roots** pressure to challenge segregation. This took a variety of forms.

The NAACP and legal campaigns

The American legal system was designed to protect the constitutional rights of American citizens. The rights of citizens are set out in the **Bill of Rights**. Courts have the legal power to uphold the rights of citizens in cases where they are under threat. Discussions made in lower courts can be challenged in higher courts. The Supreme Court's decisions, however, are final.

The National Association for the Advancement of Colored People (**NAACP**) used the American legal system to challenge segregation by appealing to the constitutional rights of black citizens. Their legal team included Thurgood Marshall, who became the first black American Supreme Court Justice in 1967.

The NAACP ran a series of **court cases** in the decade following the Second World War that appealed to the rights set out in the American Constitution in order to show that segregation was illegal.

Case	Date	Supreme Court ruling
Smith v. Allwright	1944	Black citizens had a right to vote in **primary elections**.
Morgan v. Virginia	1946	Segregation on **interstate** transport was illegal.
Sweatt v. Painter	1950	Graduate education provision must be desegregated.

The Journey of Reconciliation, 1947

The NAACP's *de jure* victories did not always lead to *de facto* change. In 1947, the civil rights organisation **CORE** launched a campaign called 'The Journey of Reconciliation'. The campaign was designed to test how far the ruling of *Morgan v. Virginia* had been implemented. Sixteen members of CORE travelled on interstate buses from the Northern states to the Southern states. On the journey, twelve activists were arrested for sitting in the 'wrong' part of the bus. In this way, the two-week campaign demonstrated that the Supreme Court ruling was being ignored and that *de jure* victories had little *de facto* impact.

> ### *De jure* and *de facto* change
> - *De jure* change describes a change in the law. It does not necessarily mean a change in practice.
> - *De facto* change describes a change in practice.

Direct action

In addition to court cases and test rulings, a collection of local civil rights groups engaged in boycotts and **pickets** in order to challenge racism. For example, in 1947, the NAACP organised a picket of department stores in New Orleans. These stores had refused to allow black customers to try on hats. Later, in 1951, the NAACP organised school boycotts in protest against inequality in education. Additionally, in 1953, the **UDL** organised a seven-day bus boycott in Louisiana. The campaign was too short to force the desegregation of the buses.

Voting campaigns

Between 1940 and 1947, **CNO** organised a voter registration campaign in Arkansas. The proportion of black Americans registered to vote increased from 1.5 per cent to 17.3 per cent.

Mind map

Use the information in Section 1 so far to add detail to the mind map below.

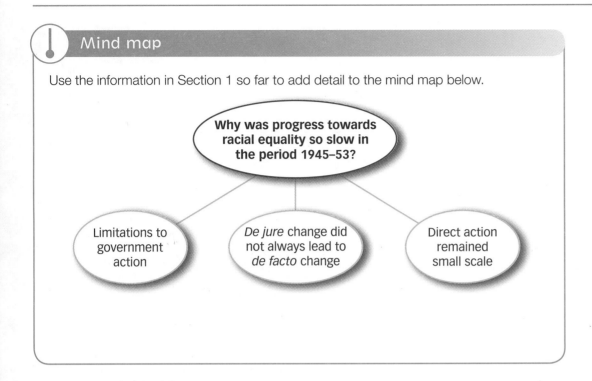

Simple essay style

Below is a sample exam question. Use your own knowledge and the information on the opposite page to produce a plan for this question. Choose four general points, and provide three pieces of specific information to support each general point. Once you have planned your essay, write the introduction and conclusion for the essay. The introduction should list the points to be discussed in the essay. The conclusion should summarise the key points and justify which point was the most important.

'The NAACP's campaigns in the years 1945 to 1953 were a failure because they did not bring about racial equality.' How far do you agree with this view?

Spectrum of significance

Below are a sample exam-style question and a list of general points that could be used to answer the question. Use your own knowledge and the information on the opposite page to reach a judgement about the importance of these general points to the question posed. Write numbers on the spectrum below to indicate their relative importance. Then write a brief justification of your placement, explaining why some of these factors are more important than others. The resulting diagram could form the basis of an essay plan.

Why was progress towards racial equality so slow in the period 1945–53?

1. Limitations to government action.
2. *De jure* change did not always lead to *de facto* change.
3. Direct action remained small scale.

Very important ←——————————————————————→ Less important

9

The NAACP'S education campaigns

Revised

Having won the 1950 court case *Sweatt v. Painter*, the NAACP extended its education campaigns.

The importance of education

The NAACP targeted education because it was possible to show that current practice was illegal. *Plessy v. Ferguson* ruled that segregation was legal as long as segregated facilities were equal. In schools, it was possible to compare class sizes, resource levels and state funding to show inequalities in provision for black and white children. For example, classes in white schools were one-third smaller than those in black schools.

The Brown case, 1954

In 1954, the NAACP went to court in support of black schoolgirl Linda Brown. Brown lived five blocks from an all-white school, but twenty blocks from her all-black school. The NAACP argued that she was at a disadvantage to white students who could attend a local school. The Supreme Court ruled in Brown's favour, stating that education should be desegregated.

However, the impact of the Brown ruling was limited because it did not draw up a timetable for this desegregation. Therefore, there was little immediate change.

Brown II, 1955

Due to the limitations of the Brown I ruling, the NAACP went back to court. This time, the Supreme Court ruled that desegregation in education should occur 'with all deliberate speed'. Again, it failed to specify exactly when desegregation of education should occur.

White reactions to the Brown case

Group	Reaction
Southern whites	'White backlash' – middle-class Southern whites set up White Citizens' Councils to oppose desegregation of schools. By 1956, these had 250,000 members.
Ku Klux Klan	There was an increase in KKK violence. For example, in 1955, the KKK lynched Emmett Till, a 14-year-old black boy accused of flirting with a white woman.
Politicians	• Senator Harry F. Byrd and 100 other Southern Congressmen issued the Southern Manifesto, which called for 'massive resistance' against desegregation. • Republican President Dwight D. Eisenhower (1953–61) refused to publically endorse the Brown decisions. In private, he felt that black campaigners wanted too much, too fast.

The significance of the Brown case

The Brown rulings were significant for the following reasons.

■ Brown I outlawed racial segregation in public education facilities. It argued that separate education could never truly be equal, ending the doctrine of 'separate but equal' established by *Plessy v. Ferguson*. By overturning *Plessy v. Ferguson*, the ruling undermined the legal basis for segregation.

■ Brown I and Brown II demonstrated that the Supreme Court was sympathetic to civil rights, but reluctant to enforce a timeframe for change. In this sense, *de jure* change did not lead to significant *de facto* change.

■ Reactions to the Brown cases showed the extent of white opposition to desegregation.

The impact of the Brown cases

The Brown decisions did not lead to widespread or immediate desegregation. Indeed, by 1957, 97 per cent of black students in the Southern states remained in segregated schools.

Develop the detail

Below are a sample exam-style question and a paragraph written in answer to this question. The paragraph contains a limited amount of detail. Annotate the paragraph to add additional detail to the answer.

How far do you agree that the Brown case was the most significant achievement in the campaign for racial equality in the period 1945–55?

The Brown case was a very significant achievement in the campaign for racial equality in the period 1945–55. For example, the case overturned the ruling that had justified segregation for many years. It also showed that the Supreme Court was sympathetic to the campaign. However, white people reacted badly to the ruling. Also, the change in the law did not lead to a change in reality. Despite this, the Brown case was very significant because it overturned the legal basis for segregation.

Simple essay style

Below is a sample exam-style question. Use your own knowledge and the information on the opposite page to produce a plan for an answer to this question. Choose four general points, and provide three pieces of specific information to support each point. Once you have planned your essay, write the introduction and conclusion for the essay. The introduction should list the points to be discussed in the essay. The conclusion should summarise the key points and justify which point was the most important.

How far do you agree that the legal campaigns of the NAACP were the most significant reason for progress towards racial equality in the period 1945–55?

Slow progress

During the decade after the Second World War, there were many signs of change. In spite of this, progress towards racial equality was slow. There were several reasons for this.

Presidential support

Truman (President 1945–53)

Truman was committed to advancing civil rights. He used his power to desegregate the armed forces as well as establishing the President's Committee on Civil Rights. However, he did not introduce all of the recommendations made in 'To Secure These Rights'. Indeed, towards the end of his presidency he was preoccupied by the Korean War and therefore did not give civil rights the attention it deserved.

Eisenhower (President 1953–61)

Eisenhower took the view that racial prejudice could not be overturned by passing laws. He believed that racism would die out naturally over time. He was critical of black campaigners, who, in his view, made unrealistic demands in an aggressive manner. Essentially, Eisenhower did not think that it was his job to tackle racial discrimination in America.

The Supreme Court

Between 1945 and 1955 the Supreme Court consistently ruled in favour of black rights. Supreme Court Justice Earl Warren, who was appointed to the Supreme Court in 1953, was particularly sympathetic to civil rights. In fact, Warren was behind the Brown ruling of 1954. Nonetheless, in 1955 the Supreme Court refused to set a legally binding timetable to enforce desegregation. Moreover, it was powerless to turn its *de jure* decisions into *de facto* change.

Congress

In the decade following the Second World War, **Congress** took no steps to change the law in favour of America's black citizens. This is because Southern Democrats, who were sometimes called **Dixiecrats**, were powerful enough in the **Senate** and the **House of Representatives** to block any civil rights legislation. Moreover, the presidents were unwilling to propose significant civil rights legislation because they needed the support of Southern Democrats to pass other pieces of legislation.

Truman came under fire from Dixiecrats in his party during the 1948 presidential election. Indeed, J. Strom Thurmond, a Southern Democrat, put himself forward as a Dixiecrat candidate against Truman because of Truman's public endorsement of civil rights. Finally, the Southern Manifesto is evidence of Congress' opposition to racial integration.

White opinion

The backlash that followed the Brown decision indicates the extent of racism in the Southern states. The Brown ruling, which led to very little immediate change, enraged Southern racists who organised White Citizens' Councils to resist change by all legal means. What is more, the killing of Emmett Till indicated that some whites were willing to use illegal, violent means to preserve segregation in the South.

Conclusion

Progress towards racial equality was slow in the decade following the Second World War because opposition to change was far stronger than support for racial equality. The Brown decisions were a significant *de jure* victory because they undermined the legal basis for segregation. However, *de facto* change was slow to come.

Support or challenge?

Below is a sample exam-style question that asks how far you agree with a specific statement. Below this are a series of general statements that are relevant to the question. Using your own knowledge and the information on the opposite page, decide whether these statements support or challenge the statement in the question and tick the appropriate box.

How accurate is it to say that there was significant progress towards racial equality in the period 1945–55?

Position(s)	SUPPORT	CHALLENGE
Many black Americans migrated North during the Second World War.		
President Truman desegregated the army.		
The President's Committee on Civil Rights published a report called 'To Secure These Rights'.		
President Truman desegregated the canteen at Washington Airport.		
Morgan v. Virginia outlawed segregation on interstate transport.		
The Brown case overturned *Plessy v. Ferguson*.		
Emmett Till was murdered by the KKK.		
Presidential initiatives were not supported by Congress.		

Complex essay style

Below are a sample exam-style question, a list of key points to be made in the essay, and a simple introduction and conclusion for the essay. Read the question, the key points and the introduction and conclusion. Rewrite the introduction and the conclusion in order to develop an argument.

Why was progress made towards racial equality in the period 1945–55?

Key points

- The Second World War
- Presidential action
- Early direct action campaigns
- NAACP legal campaigns

Introduction

There were four key reasons why progress was made towards racial equality in the period 1945–55. These were the Second World War, presidential action, early direct action campaigns and the NAACP legal campaigns.

Conclusion

There were four key reasons why progress was made towards racial equality in the period 1945–55. The most important reason was the NAACP legal campaigns. These played a more significant role than all of the other factors.

Recommended reading

Below is a list of suggested further reading on this topic.

- William H. Chafe, Raymond Gavins and Robert Korstad (eds.), *Remembering Jim Crow* (The New Press, 2008), pages 1–22.
- Jennifer Lynn Ritterhouse, *Growing Up With Jim Crow* (Chapel Hill, 2006), pages 1–21.
- Vivienne Sanders, *Civil Rights in the USA 1945–1968* (Hodder Education, 2008), pages 32–62.

Exam Focus

Below is a sample A-grade essay. Read the essay and the examiner's comments around it.

How accurate is it to say that there was no change in the position of black Americans in the period 1945–55?

The introduction immediately focuses on the question.

The essay distinguishes between *de jure* and *de facto* and between North and South.

> It is not very accurate to say that there was no *de jure* change in the position of black Americans in the period 1945–55. The biggest *de jure* change was the Brown case, which ended the legal basis for segregation in the Southern states. However, there was much less change in the *de facto* position of black Americans. Nonetheless, this period saw the beginnings of change, as the status of black people changed due to the Second World War, the actions of President Truman and most importantly, the early campaigns of the civil rights movement.

This paragraph uses dates accurately to show thorough knowledge of the topic.

> Between 1945 and 1955 there was a significant amount of legal change in the position of black Americans. *Morgan v. Virginia*, a court case of 1946, established that segregation on interstate transport was illegal. In 1950, *Sweatt v. Painter* achieved the desegregation of some graduate education. However, the most important case was the Brown case of 1954. Segregation was based on the Supreme Court ruling *Plessy v. Ferguson* of 1896. This established the principle of 'separate but equal', meaning that it was legal to force people to use segregated facilities as long as they were equally good. The Brown case changed this, because the Supreme Court argued that segregation meant that people were not treated equally. In this way, not only did the Brown case outlaw segregation in education, it also caused a significant change in the position of black people more generally because it ended the *de jure* basis of segregation.

This paragraph balances the previous paragraph by highlighting limitations in the level of change.

> However, *de facto* change in the position of black Americans was slow. During the Journey of Reconciliation of 1947, activists from CORE travelled on interstate buses to see if the legal victory that the NAACP had won in the case *Morgan v. Virginia* in 1946 had led to real change. Of the sixteen members of CORE who travelled on the buses, twelve were arrested. The two-week campaign showed that there had been little change. Similarly, the Brown case, which concerned education, did not lead to the immediate desegregation of schools in the South. Even two years after Brown II, which ordered that schools should desegregate 'with all deliberate speed', 97 per cent of black students in the South were still in segregated schools. Clearly, *de jure* change did not lead to *de facto* change because the Supreme Court's decisions were not effectively enforced.

> Even so, the status of black people did change across America. During the Second World War 500,000 black workers from the

Southern states migrated to the Northern states in search of work. In the North, black workers received better wages than they had done in the South. What is more, it was easier to vote and therefore, black people in the North were able to elect black politicians. Additionally, many black soldiers were welcomed home as heroes. For example, black fighter pilot Woodrow Crockett was recognised as one of the best American pilots of the war. The improving status of black people led President Truman to publically address the issue of civil rights. Truman set up the President's Committee on Civil Rights, which published a report in 1947 entitled 'To Secure These Rights'. The report recommended ending segregation. Truman never fulfilled this, but the impact of the war and the President's efforts both show that the status of black people was improving because in the North they had greater political power and greater wealth than before the war.

Finally, and most importantly, black people were beginning to organise to fight for their own rights. The NAACP spearheaded a series of legal campaigns, as well as organising pickets of department stores in New Orleans in 1947. CORE launched the Journey of Reconciliation in 1947. The UDL organised a week-long boycott of the buses in Louisiana in 1953. Significantly, CNO ran a voter registration campaign in the state of Arkansas, successfully increasing the proportion of black Americans registered to vote from 1.5 per cent in 1940 to 17.3 per cent in 1947. Although these campaigns did not overturn racial discrimination, they were highly significant in improving the position of black people because they demonstrated that black Americans were organising against racism.

It is clearly not very accurate to say that there was no change in the position of black Americans in the period 1945–55. The Second World War led to notable improvements in the status of black people, and notable political and economic changes. Furthermore, the actions of President Truman indicated that the Federal Government had recognised its responsibility to address racism. Most importantly, black people had shown the impact of organised protest, ending the legal basis of segregation. In this sense, this period saw a significant change in the de jure position of black Americans, even if the de facto change was less substantial.

This paragraph extends the range of material discussed in the essay by shifting focus to the Northern states and to the issues of status.

These statistics are accurate and detailed and increase the level of detail in the essay overall.

The conclusion presents a focused summary of the argument of the essay, returning to the issues of de jure and de facto change.

30/30

This essay presents a sustained and analytical account of the changing position of black Americans in the decade after the Second World War. The frequent distinctions between de jure and de facto change, and between conditions in the North and the South, mean that this essay is awarded a mark in Level 5. Equally, the excellent range and level of detail allow the essay to score highly within Level 5.

Reverse engineering

The best essays are based on careful plans. Read the essay and the examiner's comments and try to work out the general points of the plan used to write the essay. Once you have done this, note down the specific examples used to support each general point.

Section 2:
Martin Luther King and peaceful protest, 1955–68

The Montgomery Bus Boycott and the Little Rock campaign

Revised

The period 1955–68 is generally recognised as the highpoint of the modern **civil rights movement**. Many of the campaigns were inspired by Martin Luther King's commitment to **peaceful protest**.

Martin Luther King and peaceful protest

King's philosophy was inspired by **Gandhi** and **Jesus**. Essentially, he believed that peaceful protest would demonstrate the dignity of the protestors and highlight the barbaric nature of the racists opposed to civil rights. In this sense, peaceful protest would put moral pressure on the authorities to recognise the civil rights of black Americans.

The Montgomery Bus Boycott, 1955–56

In December 1955, **Rosa Parks** was arrested for refusing to give up her seat to a white passenger on a segregated bus. Local activists immediately organised a bus boycott in protest at segregation on the buses. At the same time, the **NAACP** fought a **court case**, *Browder v. Gayle* (1956), which challenged the legality of segregation on public transport.

The boycott lasted for just over a year, during which time 85 per cent of Montgomery's black **citizens** refused to use the buses.

Achievements

The NAACP case, *Browder v. Gayle*, was successful as it established that segregation on public transport was illegal. The Montgomery Bus Company officially desegregated their buses on 21 December 1956.

The Little Rock campaign, 1957

The Brown rulings had established that school segregation was illegal. However, this *de jure* change had led to little *de facto* progress. In 1957, nine black students, backed by the NAACP, attempted to enrol in the all-white Little Rock High School in Arkansas. The students were prevented from enrolling by a white mob and by the **National Guard**, who were called in by Orval Faubus, Governor of Arkansas.

Following media attention, President Eisenhower ordered the National Guard to protect the students and to allow them to enrol. Faubus responded by closing all schools in Little Rock claiming that desegregation would lead to racist violence.

Achievements

The NAACP challenged the closure of schools in the court case *Cooper v. Aaron* (1958). The **Supreme Court** ruled in the NAACP's favour, arguing that it was illegal to prevent desegregation for any reason.

Significance of the Montgomery Bus Boycott

- The boycott highlighted the economic power of black Americans: during the boycott the revenue of the bus company fell by $250,000.

- It attracted a great deal of favourable media attention, which put pressure on the bus company to change.

- The boycott demonstrated the effectiveness of coupling peaceful protest and legal action.

- It launched the career of Martin Luther King, and resulted in the foundation of a new civil rights organisation, the Southern Christian Leadership Conference (**SCLC**).

Significance of the Little Rock campaign

- The protest showed the effectiveness of using peaceful protest to test Supreme Court rulings, ensuring that *de jure* change led to *de facto* change.

- It forced Eisenhower to intervene in defence of civil rights.

- It showed the lengths to which white racists would go to prevent desegregation.

Below are a sample exam-style question and a paragraph written in answer to this question. Read the paragraph and decide which option (in bold) is most appropriate. Delete the least appropriate options and complete the paragraph by justifying your selection.

How far do you agree that peaceful protest was the main reason for the progress towards racial equality in the years 1955–68?

Early peaceful protest campaigns were **extremely/moderately/not very** significant in progress towards racial equality. For example, in the early years of the period, Martin Luther King headed the Montgomery Bus Boycott of 1955–56. This campaign proved the enormous economic power of black Americans. It proved that the media could be sympathetic to civil rights, and it led to the emergence of Martin Luther King as a national figure. Equally, the Little Rock campaign of 1957, in which nine students asserted their right to enrol in Little Rock High School, was significant because it forced President Eisenhower to support a campaign for desegregation. In this way, early peaceful protests were **extremely/moderately/not very** significant in progress towards racial equality because

_____

_____

Below are a sample exam-style question and a paragraph written in answer to this question. Read the paragraph and identify parts that are not directly relevant to the question. Draw a line through the information that is irrelevant and justify your deletions in the margin.

How far had racial equality been achieved by 1957?

In the area of education, some progress had been made towards racial equality by 1955. In 1954, the NAACP took the Brown case to the Supreme Court. The NAACP used court cases to campaign for greater rights for black Americans. The Supreme Court was America's highest court of law. People took cases to the Supreme Court when they believed that their rights, as set out in the American Constitution, had been violated. The NAACP's Brown case resulted in the ruling that segregation in education was illegal. This overturned the ruling of *Plessy v. Ferguson*, which had been the result of a case brought to the Supreme Court by a man called Homer Plessy. Despite the significance of the Brown ruling, the case failed to create widespread change. Indeed, even following Brown II — which ruled that change should occur 'with all deliberate speed' — and the Little Rock campaign, which sought to speed up school desegregation, change was slow to occur. By 1957, 97 per cent of black students in the Southern states remained in segregated schools. This problem continued throughout the 1960s, and is one reason why racial equality had not been achieved by 1968.

The Greensboro sit-ins and the Freedom Rides

Revised

The Greensboro sit-ins, 1960

In 1960, inspired by King, four black students attempted to force the desegregation of a lunch-counter in a Woolworth's store. The students, who were based in Greensboro, North Carolina, staged a **sit-in**, which lasted for several days. By the fourth day, 300 students had joined the sit-in, and by the end of the week the store had closed the lunch-counter rather than desegregate. The Greensboro sit-in inspired similar sit-ins across the **Southern states**. Many of these protests were organised by the SCLC.

Achievements

- The Greensboro Woolworth's store was desegregated in May 1960.
- By the beginning of 1962, 70,000 people, black and white, had taken part in some kind of protest against segregation.
- Consequently, by the end of 1961, 810 towns in the Southern states had desegregated public places.

Significance of the sit-ins

- The success of the sit-ins led to the foundation of a new organisation – the Student Non-violent Co-ordinating Committee (**SNCC**).

- The protests demonstrated continuing media interest in the campaign for civil rights.

- They highlighted the economic power of black Americans: Woolworth's profits decreased by one-third during the protests.

- They showed the widespread willingness of young black people to stand up for their rights.

- Eisenhower publicly expressed support for those campaigning for greater civil rights.

The Freedom Rides, 1961

The 1946 case, *Morgan v. Virginia*, had ruled that **interstate** transport should be desegregated. However, the case had made no judgment about interstate transport facilities such as waiting rooms. Therefore, the NAACP returned to court in 1960 in the case *Boynton v. Virginia* to force the desegregation of interstate transport facilities.

Both cases resulted in *de jure* victories, but little immediate *de facto* change. Inspired by the Journey of Reconciliation, **CORE** mounted the Freedom Rides, a campaign to test these rulings. During the campaign, seven black and six white activists took bus journeys across the South, encountering enormous white violence in the form of beatings and firebombs. King spoke out against the violence, and in support of the Freedom Riders.

Achievements

- The **Federal Government** promised to enforce the desegregation of interstate buses and bus facilities.
- By September 1961, all signs enforcing segregation had been removed from interstate transport.

Significance of the Freedom Rides

- The Rides demonstrated unity between civil rights organisations. CORE, SNCC and the SCLC all contributed to the campaign.

- The violent reaction to the protest forced President John F. Kennedy to act, but demonstrated his reluctance to support direct action. He initially refused to protect the protestors, instead offering them grants to abandon their campaign in favour of a voter registration drive. After the protest, Kennedy asked for a period of 'cooling off', by which he meant an end to direct action campaigns.

Complete the paragraph
(a)

Below are a sample exam-style question and a paragraph written in answer to this question. The paragraph contains a point and a concluding explanatory link back to the question, but lacks examples. Complete the paragraph by adding this link in the space provided.

Why was so much achieved by the civil rights movement in the period 1955–61?

> The civil rights movement achieved a great deal because of its policy of non-violent direct action. For example,
>
> _____
>
> _____
>
> Clearly, non-violent direct action was a very effective tool in advancing civil rights because it gained media attention and the sympathy of white opinion in the North.

Identify an argument
(a)

Below are a series of definitions, a sample exam-style question and two sample conclusions. One of the conclusions achieves a high level because it contains an argument. The other achieves a lower level because it contains only description and assertion. Identify which is which. The mark scheme on page 3 will help you.

- **Description:** a detailed account.
- **Assertion:** a statement of fact or an opinion that is not supported by a reason.
- **Reason:** a statement that explains or justifies something.
- **Argument:** an assertion justified with a reason.

Why was so much achieved by the civil rights movement in the period 1955–61?

Sample 1

> In conclusion, the civil rights movement achieved so much in the period 1955–61 because the focus had shifted from *de jure* change to *de facto* change. During the 1940s and early 1950s, the NAACP had won important *de jure* victories. However, it was mainly after 1955 that black campaigners harnessed the power of peaceful protest to force the authorities to implement *de facto* change. This was certainly the case in the Montgomery Bus Boycott, Little Rock, the sit-ins and the Freedom Rides.

Sample 2

> In conclusion, the civil rights movement achieved much in the period 1955–61. The Montgomery Bus Boycott was a big success because it forced desegregation on the buses in Montgomery. Little Rock forced the state of Arkansas to proceed with educational desegregation. The sit-in movement achieved desegregation of public places. Finally, the Freedom Rides forced the desegregation of interstate transport and transport facilities. Overall, peaceful protest achieved a great deal through a large number of very successful campaigns.

From Albany to Birmingham

Civil rights campaigns from 1955 to 1961 had achieved great things. The Albany campaign, however, was the movement's first major failure. Nonetheless, King refused to be beaten. He learnt from his mistakes and mounted the Birmingham campaign of 1963, the civil rights movement's greatest success to date.

The Albany campaign, 1961–62

In 1961, the SCLC organised protests against segregation in Albany, Georgia. However, the campaign was unsuccessful because local police chief, Laurie Pritchett, had studied the methods of previous civil rights campaigns and had developed a strategy for dealing with them.

Essentially, Pritchett realised that white violence against black protestors led to media attention, which forced changed. Therefore, Pritchett instructed the local police to treat protestors with respect. In so doing, he prevented violence and denied the protestors the media attention they needed. Pritchett even paid King's bail after he was arrested, in order to ensure that King could not capitalise on his arrest in the media.

Achievements

At the end of the campaign, Pritchett made vague promises to end segregation, but subsequently took action to ensure that his desegregation measures were meaningless. For example, desegregated parks were closed and chairs were removed from desegregated libraries.

Significance of the Albany campaign

- The campaign demonstrated the importance of gaining media attention – without this, the campaigners could not force effective change.

- The campaign led to divisions within the civil rights movement. Some **radicals** in SNCC began to argue in favour of abandoning the strategy of non-violence.

The Birmingham campaign, 1963

Following the failure of the Albany campaign, King and the SCLC targeted Birmingham, Alabama. Eugene 'Bull' Connor, the local police chief, had reacted violently to the Freedom Rides and therefore King believed a campaign in Birmingham would lead to violence and therefore media attention.

The SCLC also made the decision to recruit children and students, and to place them in the front line of marches and demonstrations. As expected, the local police responded with violence, using water cannon and setting dogs on protestors.

Achievements

The SCLC successfully negotiated the desegregation of Birmingham's department stores and a commitment to end racial discrimination in employment. Media coverage of police violence shocked America and the world, forcing Kennedy to publicly back a **bill** to end segregation once and for all.

Significance of the Birmingham campaign

- The **Soviet Union** devoted one-fifth of its news coverage to the protest, which was highly embarrassing for America in the context of the **Cold War**.

- The campaign, and international reaction, convinced Kennedy of the need for a civil rights act.

- Media coverage and King's '**Letter from Birmingham Jail**' won enormous white support, particularly in the North, for the civil rights campaign.

- Divisions among **civil rights groups** intensified: the SCLC was criticised for putting children in harm's way during the campaign.

- White violence continued after the campaign: the **KKK** bombed a black church in Birmingham, killing four young girls.

Below are a sample exam-style question and a paragraph written in answer to this question. Why does this paragraph not get into Level 4? Once you have identified the mistake, rewrite the paragraph so that it displays the qualities of Level 4. The mark scheme on page 3 will help you.

How significant was Martin Luther King in the campaign for racial equality in the period 1955–63?

Martin Luther King came to public attention in the Montgomery Bus Boycott of 1955–56. In 1955 a woman named Rosa Parks sat on a bus and refused to give up her seat to a white person. She was later fined for this and Martin Luther King was elected as leader of the Montgomery Improvement Association. In this role, he led the black community of Montgomery in a bus boycott, which lasted a year, and forced the authorities to desegregate the buses in Montgomery. After the Montgomery Bus Boycott, King founded the Southern Christian Leadership Conference, which went on to run the Albany campaign of 1961–62 and the Birmingham campaign of 1963. The Albany campaign was not very successful. Police Chief Laurie Pritchett made sure there was no violence and so the campaign did not get media attention. The Birmingham campaign was much more successful. 'Bull' Connor, Birmingham's police chief, was violent and therefore the media were interested. It was King's most successful campaign to date.

Below are a sample exam-style question and a paragraph written in answer to this question. Read the paragraph and identify parts that are not directly relevant to the question. Draw a line through the information that is irrelevant and justify your deletions in the space at the bottom of the page.

How significant was Martin Luther King in the campaign for racial equality in the period 1955–63?

King was not the only important factor; other civil rights groups also played an important role. CORE was founded in 1941 and its support grew during the war as black pride and status improved. In 1947, CORE ran the Journey of Reconciliation to test the ruling *Morgan v. Virginia*. In 1961, CORE took to the buses again in the Freedom Rides, this time testing the 1960 ruling *Boynton v. Virginia*. CORE played a significant role in this regard, as the protest showed that *de jure* change had not led to *de facto* change. What is more, the Freedom Rides forced President Kennedy to oversee the desegregation of interstate transport and transport facilities, another important victory for the movement. Kennedy became president in 1961, but only governed until his assassination in 1963. The NAACP was also important in forcing *de jure* change. For example, they were involved in the court cases *Sweatt v. Painter, Browder v. Gayle, Cooper v. Aaron* and *Boynton v. Virginia*. These court cases further undermined the legality of segregation. In this way, CORE and the NAACP played an important role in the campaign for racial equality because, through legal challenges and non-violent protest, they rolled back segregation in the South.

The March on Washington and the Civil Rights Act of 1964

Revised

The March on Washington, 1963

The SCLC, SNCC, CORE and the NAACP all worked together to organise a march commemorating the one hundredth anniversary of the end of slavery. A quarter of a million people, 50,000 of whom were white, marched to the Lincoln Memorial in Washington, where King made his famous 'I have a dream' speech.

Achievements

The March on Washington forced Kennedy to make good on his promise and begin work on a Civil Rights Act. The peaceful nature of the march also led to a great deal of positive media coverage. Finally, civil rights leaders, including King, began working closely with the Federal Government during the campaign.

Significance of the March on Washington

- The March demonstrated the unity of the civil rights movement in its call for desegregation.
- Positive media attention ensured sustained white support for desegregation.
- Kennedy had been reluctant to permit the March, fearing that it would become violent. King assured Kennedy that it would remain peaceful, persuading Kennedy to back the march. In this way, it demonstrated that the President held King in high regard.

The Civil Rights Act, 1964

Why was the Act passed?

- Civil rights campaigns had gained media attention and public support, particularly in the Northern states.
- Kennedy's assassination in 1963 increased public sympathy for the Act. His successor, President Lyndon B. Johnson, said that the Act would be a fitting legacy for Kennedy.
- The 1964 Congressional elections had replaced many **Dixiecrats** with more liberal Democrats, who were sympathetic to civil rights.
- The new president threw his weight behind the bill, persuading senior members of **Congress** to back it.

The provisions of the Act

- The Civil Rights Act outlawed all segregation of public facilities or places.
- It established the Commission on Civil Rights, which was empowered to enforce desegregation.
- It outlawed racial discrimination in employment.

The effectiveness of the Act

Successes	Limitations
• Between 1964 and 1968, the Act was used to force 53 cities to desegregate. • By 1968, black unemployment was seven per cent, not far above white unemployment, which stood at five per cent. • Over the next decade, it led to the wholesale dismantling of segregation in the South.	• By 1968, 58 per cent of Southern black schoolchildren remained in segregated schools. • By 1968, the average income of black workers was still only 61 per cent of the average income of white workers. • It did not address inequalities in the provision of housing. • It did not address black voting rights.

Significance of the Civil Rights Act

- The Civil Rights Act was extremely significant because it gave the Government the power to enforce desegregation across the South. In this sense, it was simultaneously a *de jure* and a *de facto* victory for the civil rights movement.

Simple essay style

Below is a sample exam-style question. Use your own knowledge and the information on the opposite page to produce a plan for an answer to this question. Choose four general points, and provide three pieces of specific information to support each point. Once you have planned your essay, write the introduction and conclusion for the essay. The introduction should list the points to be discussed in the essay. The conclusion should summarise the key points and justify which point was the most important.

How far do you agree that peaceful protest was the main reason for the passing of the 1964 Civil Rights Act?

Support or challenge?

Below is a sample exam-style question, which asks how far you agree with a specific statement. Below this are a series of general statements, which are relevant to the question. Using your own knowledge and the information on the opposite page, decide whether these statements support or challenge the statement in the question and tick the appropriate box.

'The passing of the 1964 Civil Rights Act brought racial equality to America.' How far do you agree with this statement?

Position(s)	SUPPORT	CHALLENGE
The 1964 Civil Rights Act outlawed segregation across the Southern states.		
The 1964 Civil Rights Act empowered the Commission on Civil Rights to enforce desegregation.		
Legal segregation did not affect black Americans in the North.		
Unemployment among black people was two per cent greater than unemployment among white people.		
The Civil Rights Act did not lead to voting reform.		
Many white Americans believed that the Civil Rights Act effectively solved the problem of racism in America.		
Between 1964 and 1974, segregation was dismantled across the South.		
The Civil Rights Act sped up the pace of desegregation.		

Voting rights, 1957–65

Revised

The struggle for enfranchisement

Segregation in the South went hand in hand with widespread **disenfranchisement**. Between 1957 and 1965 there was a series of attempts to increase the number of black voters in the Southern states.

Voter registration under Eisenhower

Eisenhower proposed two Civil Rights Acts focusing on voting rights.

The 1957 Civil Rights Act

Eisenhower's first Act established a Commission on Civil Rights to monitor the voting rights of black Americans. Individuals found guilty of preventing black Americans from voting would face a fine of $1,000 or six months in jail.

However, the Act's impact was limited because all-white juries in the South were unlikely to convict corrupt local officials

The 1960 Civil Rights Act

Eisenhower's second Act extended the powers of the Commission on Civil Rights by requiring local authorities to keep records of voter registration. These could be checked by the Commission.

Eisenhower's Acts only increased the proportion of black voters by three per cent. By 1963, only 800,000 of the South's 20 million black citizens were registered to vote.

The effectiveness of Eisenhower's Acts was hindered by Southern Democrats in Congress who staged **filibusters** to try to block the bills.

The Mississippi Freedom Summer, 1964

The Mississippi Freedom Summer was a campaign that focused on voting rights. Around 800 activists from SNCC, CORE and SCLC targeted Mississippi, a state where only 6.2 per cent of black adults were registered to vote. During the campaign, 17,000 black people tried to register to vote, but due to white opposition only 1,600 succeeded.

The Selma campaign, 1965

Voting rights were also addressed by the Selma campaign. SCLC and SNCC organisers planned to lead a march between Selma, Alabama and Montgomery to mark the tenth anniversary of the bus boycott. However, the first attempt to lead the march failed due to police intervention. The second attempt was stopped shortly after Johnson appealed directly to King to call a halt to the march. On the third attempt, 25,000 protestors successfully completed the march.

The march showed continuing unity between SCLC and SNCC, as well as demonstrating King's good relationship with Johnson. Indeed, following the march, Johnson proposed the Voting Rights Act to Congress. Nonetheless, King was criticised by black radicals for giving in to Johnson's request to delay the march.

The Voting Rights Act, 1965

The Voting Rights Act was significant for the following reasons.

- It outlawed all tests and clauses that prevented American citizens from voting, such as the **literacy test** and **grandfather clauses**.
- It gave the Federal Government the power to oversee voter registration across America.

The impact of the Voting Rights Act

- Between 1965 and 1966, 230,000 black people registered to vote across the Southern states.
- More black people were elected to government positions. For example, in 1967, Richard G. Hatcher was elected Mayor of Gary, Indiana.
- However, by 1966, four Southern states had fewer than 50 per cent of their black citizens registered to vote.

Below are a sample exam-style question and a timeline. Read the question, study the timeline and, using three coloured pens, put a red, amber or green star next to the events to show:

- red – events and policies that have no relevance to the question
- amber – events and policies that have some significance to the question
- green – events and policies that are directly relevant to the question.

1. **Why was significant legislation to improve civil rights for black Americans passed in 1964 and 1965?**

	Greensboro sit-ins			

Above the timeline:
- Greensboro sit-ins
- Student Non-violent Co-ordinating Committee (SNCC) founded
- Southern Christian Leadership Conference (SCLC) created
- Birmingham campaign
- Mississippi Freedom Summer
- Brown II | Browder v. Gayle | (SCLC) created | Cooper v. Aaron | Civil Rights Act | Freedom Rides | Birmingham campaign | Mississippi Freedom Summer | Selma campaign

Timeline years: **1955** | **1956** | **1957** | **1958** | **1960** | **1961** | **1963** | **1964** | **1965**

Below the timeline:
- Lynching of Emmett Till
- Conclusion of the Montgomery Bus Boycott
- Civil Rights Act / Little Rock campaign
- Boynton v. Virginia
- Albany campaign begins
- March on Washington
- Civil Rights Act
- Voting Rights Act

Now repeat the activity with the following questions. You could use different colours, or number your stars 1, 2 and 3.

2. **How far had racial equality been achieved by 1965?**

3. **Why was significant legislation to improve civil rights for black Americans not passed until 1964 and 1965?**

Below are a sample exam-style question and a paragraph written in answer to this question. The paragraph contains a limited amount of detail. Annotate the paragraph to add additional detail to the answer.

How far had racial equality been achieved by 1965?

In the area of voting, significant progress had been made by 1965. For example, even though Eisenhower's Civil Rights Act did not add many voters to the electoral roll, the 1965 Act was much more successful. The Act had many provisions that were much more effective than previous Acts. As a result, many more black people registered to vote in the years following 1965. There were also limitations to the success of the Act. In fact, in the year after the Act, there were still a number of states where a minority of black citizens were able to vote. In this way, *de jure* racial equality had been achieved, but *de facto* equality was slower to follow.

Revised

King's Northern campaigns

King moves North

The Civil Rights Act and the Voting Rights Act spelt the end of segregation and disenfranchisement in the South. However, this legislation had little impact in the North, where the problems were economic – a fact that was highlighted in the 1965 **Moynihan Report**. Following King's successes in the South, he turned his attention to the North, hoping to address the problems of poverty in the Northern **ghettos**.

The Chicago campaign, 1966

The Chicago campaign aimed to address economic problems in employment and housing. However, a heat wave changed the focus of the campaign. Mayor Richard Daley ordered water supplies to be cut off from fire hydrants in the ghettos. Traditionally, this water had been used to cool off during hot weather. Daley's action provoked riots, which King was unable to stop. The violence forced Daley to negotiate, and he promised new laws to end discrimination in housing. However, once the SCLC left Chicago, Daley failed to make good on his promises.

Significance of the campaign

The Chicago campaign highlighted the limitations of peaceful protest.

- Chicago was ten times bigger than Birmingham. The scale of the problems facing black residents was far larger than King had anticipated.

- Church attendance was much lower in the Northern cities than in the South. Consequently, King's Christian message did not enjoy widespread support in the North.

- The political changes in the South were inexpensive to implement. However, economic change required significant funding. Johnson was preoccupied with the **Vietnam War** and unwilling to devote financial resources to civil rights.

- Northern whites had supported legal change in the Southern states. However, economic change in the North required potentially higher tax bills. For this reason, they were less sympathetic to change.

The Poor People's Campaign, 1968

King responded to the lessons of the Chicago campaign with a new initiative intended to tackle the problem of poverty throughout America. He hoped that the Poor People's Campaign would unite poor people of all races, and in so doing force the Government to address poverty across America. However, in 1967 King spoke out against the Vietnam War, alienating Johnson and ensuring that the campaign lacked presidential support. Tragically, King was assassinated before the campaign was launched.

The Memphis sanitation workers' strike, 1968

The sanitation workers' strike of 1968 united black and white workers in a campaign for better pay. King agreed to be involved because it was exactly the kind of campaign he had envisaged following his experiences in Chicago. King was assassinated during the campaign.

King's death

On 4 April 1968, King was assassinated on the balcony of his hotel in Memphis. Shortly after, James Earl Ray was convicted of his murder. King's murder led to rioting across 29 states. Stokely Carmichael, leader of the SNCC, argued that King's murder marked white America's final rejection of a peaceful solution to America's racial problems.

Use the information on the opposite page to add detail to the mind map below.

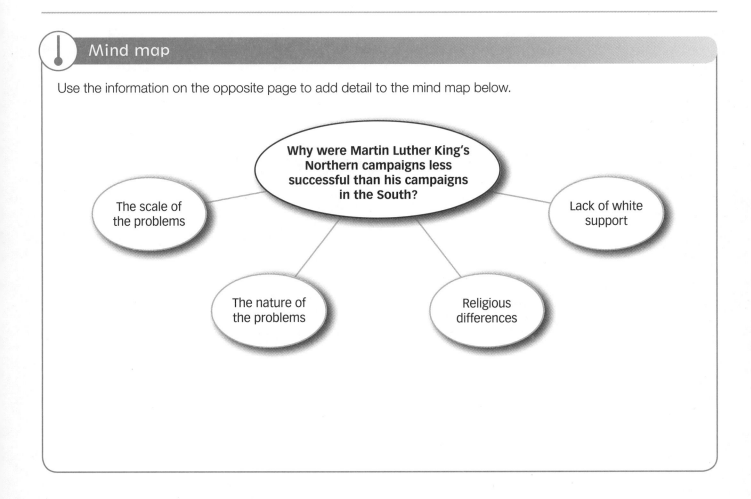

Turning assertion into argument ⓐ

Below are a sample exam-style question and a series of assertions. Read the exam-style question and then add a justification to each of the assertions to turn it into an argument.

Why were Martin Luther King's Northern campaigns less successful than his campaigns in the South?

Martin Luther King's campaigns in the North were hampered by a lack of support from Northern whites because

President Johnson was less sympathetic to King's later campaigns because

Martin Luther King had less support in Chicago's black community because

Opposition to civil rights

Revised

Political opposition

The presidents

None of the presidents publically supported segregation, but none wholeheartedly supported the methods of the civil rights movement.

Eisenhower refused to show leadership in the fight against segregation. He believed that black people needed to be patient and that change would come about naturally over time. Eisenhower did try and address the issue of black disenfranchisement. However, he was unwilling to use his authority to force Congress to pass meaningful legislation.

Kennedy was also in favour of extending black voting rights. In 1962, he set up the Voter Education Project. However, this programme was an attempt to persuade civil rights activists to abandon their own initiatives and collaborate with the Government on voter education.

Johnson believed that King's Northern campaigns were too ambitious and he refused to work with King following his criticism of America's involvement in Vietnam.

Congress

Congress opposed civil rights legislation in the following ways.

- It watered down bills – for example, the penalties for denying black citizens their right to vote established in the 1957 Civil Rights Act were reduced to a $1,000 fine or six months in jail.
- **Congressmen** filibustered to hold up legislation – for example, in 1960, eighteen Southern Dixiecrats filibustered for 125 hours in an attempt to kill Eisenhower's bill. Furthermore, during the passage of the 1964 Civil Rights Act, Senators staged a filibuster of 83 days – the longest in American history.

FBI

FBI Chief **J. Edgar Hoover** was convinced that the civil rights movement had been infiltrated by **communists** dedicated to undermining the American Government. As a result, he set up COINTELPRO to infiltrate the civil rights movement. FBI agents, pretending to be civil rights campaigners, were instructed to foster disagreement and rivalry in order to weaken the civil rights movement from within.

Local authorities

Local police chiefs used a variety of methods to hinder the civil rights movement. 'Bull' Connor, in Birmingham, used violence to try to intimidate civil rights activists. This was counter-productive as it gained the movement valuable media attention. Laurie Pritchett, on the other hand, clearly understood the importance of overt white racism and combated the movement in a more sophisticated way by ordering police officers to treat protestors with respect.

Local politicians also used different methods to deal with the campaigns. During the Little Rock campaign, Orval Faubus, Governor of Arkansas, used heavy-handed techniques such as employing the National Guard and closing schools. These were ultimately ineffective because the Federal Government was forced to act to protect the rights of the protestors. Richard Daley, Mayor of Chicago, used more subtle methods, making promises that he did not intend to keep.

Public opposition

Groups such as the KKK continued to use violence against protestors. In addition to firebombing a black church following the Birmingham campaign, the KKK were responsible for the murder of four activists and the firebombing of 30 houses during the Mississippi Freedom Summer. The North witnessed 'white flight' whereby white Americans moved out of integrated neighbourhoods, creating *de facto* segregation.

Spectrum of significance

Below are a sample exam-style question and a list of general points that could be used to answer the question. Use your own knowledge and the information on the opposite page to reach a judgement about the importance of these general points to the question posed. Write numbers on the spectrum below to indicate their relative importance. Then write a brief justification of your placement, explaining why some of these factors are more important than others. The resulting diagram could form the basis of an essay plan.

How far did opposition slow down progress towards racial equality in the period 1955–65?

1. President Eisenhower
2. President Kennedy
3. President Johnson
4. The American Congress
5. Dixiecrats
6. The FBI
7. Orval Faubus
8. Laurie Pritchett
9. 'Bull' Connor

←————————————————————————————→

To a great extent   To a small extent

Develop the detail ⓐ

Below is a sample exam-style question and a paragraph written in answer to this question. The paragraph contains a limited amount of detail. Annotate the paragraph to add additional detail to the answer.

How far did opposition slow down progress towards racial equality in the period 1955–65?

Political opposition slowed down progress towards racial equality significantly prior to 1964. For example, early civil rights bills were weakened by Congress. Congress had a variety of methods for weakening bills. The presidents also played a role in slowing progress. One president was initially unwilling to use his power to force the pace of change. Even Johnson was less helpful towards the end of the 1960s. Nonetheless, between 1964 and 1965, political opposition could not prevent the passing of two major Acts to promote racial equality. In this way, opposition did slow down progress towards racial equality, but was unable to prevent it.

Key players: King, Kennedy and Johnson

Revised

Martin Luther King

King was an inspirational and charismatic orator. His roots in the black church made him an ideal spokesman for the largely Christian Southern black community. What is more, he was able to make the case for civil rights in a way that appealed to Northern whites. He was very gifted at using the media to get his message across and his commitment to peace gave him enormous moral authority. King was also willing to work with senior politicians in his quest for civil rights.

Nonetheless, King was criticised following the Albany and Chicago campaigns for not fully grasping the nature of the problems he addressed. Additionally, lesser-known black leaders argued that the SCLC imposed its own campaigns without working with local organisations. Furthermore, some members of the SNCC accused King of treating them as the youth wing of the SCLC.

Finally, as the black movement radicalised during the 1960s, some activists described King as an '**Uncle Tom**', meaning that he was too willing to work with white authorities.

President Kennedy (President 1960–63)

Kennedy made big promises concerning civil rights during his election campaign of 1960. However, once in power, he was slow to act. His early measures were largely symbolic. For example, he appointed five black judges to federal courts and invited many black leaders to the White House. Kennedy was only willing to show decisive leadership on civil rights following the violence of the Birmingham campaign, and it was only after the March on Washington that he threw his full weight behind a civil rights bill.

President Johnson (President 1963–69)

Johnson was committed to building a 'Great Society' in which there was opportunity for all. Passing the Civil Rights Act and Voting Rights Act were part of Johnson's vision. He also backed the Elementary and Secondary Education Act (1965) and the Higher Education Act (1965). Both Acts targeted government money at the poorest schools and universities and therefore benefited many black students.

Nonetheless, Johnson's attention was diverted from the Great Society by the Vietnam War. As a result, his later record is less good. For example, the Civil Rights Act of 1968, which addressed discrimination in housing, was much less successful than his earlier Acts. Essentially, the Act outlawed racial discrimination in the sale or rental of property. However, Congress refused to support the sections of the Act that gave the Government power to enforce fair housing. As a result, it made little impact on racial discrimination in the housing market.

Complex essay style

Below are a sample exam-style question, a list of key points to be made in the essay, and a simple introduction and conclusion for the essay. Read the question, the key points, and the introduction and conclusion. Rewrite the introduction and the conclusion in order to develop an argument.

How far do you agree that the Civil Rights Act of 1964 was passed mainly due to the efforts of Martin Luther King?

Key points

- Martin Luther King
- President Kennedy
- President Johnson
- Peaceful protest

Introduction

There were four key reasons why the Civil Rights Act of 1964 was passed. These were the efforts of Martin Luther King, the role played by President Kennedy, the role played by President Johnson, and the impact of peaceful protest.

Conclusion

There were four key reasons why the Civil Rights Act of 1964 was passed. The most important reason was the efforts of Martin Luther King. These played a more significant role than all of the other factors.

You're the examiner

(a)

Below are a sample exam-style question and a paragraph written in answer to this question. Read the paragraph and the mark scheme provided on page 3. Decide which level you would award the paragraph. Write the level below, along with a justification for your choice.

How far was the contribution of Martin Luther King the most significant reason for the successes of the civil rights movement in the period 1955–65?

Martin Luther King played a significant role in the successes of the civil rights movement in the period 1955–65. For example, he led the Montgomery Bus Boycott in 1955–56. In this role, he gave inspiring speeches and encouraged black people to walk to work rather than take the bus. He was so successful that 85 per cent of Montgomery's black population boycotted the buses. Martin Luther King was also involved in the Birmingham campaign of 1963. He was arrested during this protest, and spent his time in prison writing his 'Letter from Birmingham Jail' in which he defended the use of non-violent protest. He is most famous for his role in the March on Washington in 1963, where he delivered his 'I have a dream' speech. This gained the civil rights movement a lot of publicity. Overall, therefore, Martin Luther King played a significant role in the successes of the civil rights movement in the period 1955–65 because he was at the forefront of some of the most important campaigns of the period.

Level: Reasons for choosing this level:

The achievements of peaceful protest, 1955–68

Revised

Focus	Key campaigns/legislation	Achievements
Desegregation	• Montgomery Bus Boycott (1955–56) • *Browder v. Gayle* (1956) • Little Rock (1957) • *Cooper v. Aaron* (1958) • *Boynton v. Virginia* (1960) • Greensboro sit-ins (1960) • Freedom Rides (1961) • Albany campaign (1961–62) • Birmingham campaign (1963) • March on Washington (1963) • Civil Rights Act (1964)	• The Civil Rights Act of 1964 explicitly outlawed segregation and gave the Government the power to force integration. • Prior to this, segregation on transport and in transport facilities had been declared illegal. • By 1968, only 42 per cent of black schoolchildren in Southern states attended integrated schools. • By 1965, the Civil Rights Act had been used to force the desegregation of 53 cities across the South. In total, 214 Southern cities had been desegregated.
Voting	• Civil Rights Act (1957) • Civil Rights Act (1960) • Mississippi Freedom Summer (1964) • Selma campaign (1965) • Voting Rights Act (1965)	• In total, Eisenhower's Civil Rights Acts added only three per cent more black voters to the electorate. • The Voting Rights Act of 1965 outlawed voting tests and gave the Government the power to assist black voter registration. • Between 1965 and 1966, 230,000 black people registered to vote across the South. • By 1966, only four Southern states had less than 50 per cent of their black citizens registered to vote. • In 1967, Richard G. Hatcher was elected Mayor of Gary, Indiana, and Carl B. Stokes became Mayor of Cleveland, Ohio.
Poverty	• Civil Rights Act (1964) • Elementary and Secondary Education Act (1965) • Higher Education Act (1965) • Chicago campaign (1966) • Poor People's campaign (1968) • Civil Rights Act (1968)	• There was a fourfold increase in the number of black students attending college and university during the late 1960s. • By 1968, only seven per cent of black Americans were unemployed, compared to five per cent of white Americans. • The average wage of black workers rose from 53 per cent of that of white workers in 1965, to 61 per cent in 1968. • As late as 1977, a study revealed that discrimination still occurred in 21 per cent of housing transactions.

Public support for civil rights

Public support for civil rights rose and fell in the period 1955–68. In the early 1960s, the vast majority of white Americans, particularly in the North, favoured an end to segregation. For example, a survey taken in 1964 revealed that 80 per cent of the American public supported the desegregation of education, and greater rights in employment and voting.

However, in the late 1960s, white people began 'voting with their feet', leaving parts of town with large numbers of black residents. The proportion of white citizens living in inner-city areas fell by 9.6 per cent during the 1960s. This process sped up as the decade continued, with 16.8 per cent of the urban white population leaving America's largest industrial cities in 1968 alone.

How far had equality been achieved by 1968?

By 1968, black Americans had gained full *de jure* equality with white Americans. Discrimination in education, transport, voting, housing and employment had been outlawed. Nonetheless, *de facto* change was much slower. In spite of legal change, discrimination remained a fact of life in the Northern and Southern states, and poverty was still much more widespread in black neighbourhoods than it was in largely white areas.

Delete as applicable

Below are a sample exam question and a paragraph written in answer to this question. Read the paragraph and decide which of the possible options (in bold) is most appropriate. Delete the least appropriate options and complete the paragraph by justifying your selection.

How far had racial equality been achieved by 1968?

In terms of desegregation there had been **significant/moderate/limited** progress towards racial equality by 1968. For example, segregation on transport and in transport facilities had been declared illegal by 1960. In addition, the Brown Case of 1954 had outlawed segregation in education. Most notably, the 1964 Civil Rights Act outlawed segregation across the Southern States, and gave the Government the power to enforce integration. By 1965 the Government had used this power to force the desegregation of 53 cities, bringing the total number of desegregated cities in the South to 214. However, the Civil Rights Act and the court cases that preceded it were unable to bring about complete desegregation. As late as 1968, 58 per cent of black schoolchildren in the Southern States remained in segregated schools. In this way racial equality had been achieved in terms of desegregation to a **significant/moderate/limited** degree because

_____

_____

Spectrum of significance

Below are a sample exam-style question and a list of general points that could be used to answer the question. Use your own knowledge and the information on the opposite page to reach a judgement about the importance of these points to the question posed. Write numbers on the spectrum below to indicate their relative importance. Then write a brief justification of your placement, explaining why some of these factors are more important than others. The resulting diagram could form the basis of an essay plan.

How far had racial equality been achieved by 1968?

1. Desegregation
2. Voting rights
3. Poverty
4. Public support for civil rights

⟵――――――――――――――――――――――――――⟶

Very important   Less important

Recommended reading

Below is a list of suggested further reading on this topic.

- Hugh Brogan, *The Penguin History of the United States of America* (Penguin, 1990), pages 634–665.
- Gary Gerstle, *American Crucible: Race and Nation in the Twentieth Century* (Princeton University Press, 2002), pages 268–295.
- John Howard Griffin, *Black Like Me* (Collins, 1961).

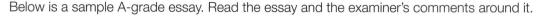

Exam focus

Revised

Below is a sample A-grade essay. Read the essay and the examiner's comments around it.

How far were the actions of the Federal Government the main reason for the advancement of civil rights in the period 1955–68?

The introduction sets up the argument that will run through the whole essay.

The actions of the Federal Government played an important part in the advancement of civil rights in the period 1955–68. Specifically, Congress' decision to pass the Civil Rights Act and the Voting Rights Act brought about an important change in the legal position of black Americans, as well as giving the Government the power to challenge segregation and disenfranchisement in the Southern states. However, for much of the period the Federal Government was not using its power to advance the rights of black Americans. Indeed, the main reason for the advancement of civil rights in the period 1955–68 was the actions of black campaigners, and their portrayal in the media.

The essay begins by focusing on the factor mentioned in the question. It provides detailed examples of Federal Government actions and the extent to which these led to change.

The federal government certainly helped to advance black rights. For example, the Civil Rights Act of 1964 made all formal racial segregation of public facilities or places illegal. Therefore it ended the power of Jim Crow laws across the South. The 1964 Act also made it illegal to discriminate racially when employing people. Importantly, the Act gave the Commission on Civil Rights the power to enforce desegregation. As a result, 53 Southern cities had been forced to desegregate their facilities by 1965. The Voting Rights Act of 1965 was also important as it addressed disenfranchisement. It made tests, such as literacy or 'general knowledge' tests, for potential voters illegal, as well as outlawing grandfather clauses. In the same way as the Civil Rights Act, it gave the Government the power to enforce the rights of black Americans who wished to register to vote. Consequently, in the year after the Act was passed, 230,000 black Americans were able to register to vote. In this way, the Federal Government played an important role in advancing civil rights because it passed Acts to end segregation and disenfranchisement and subsequently enforced them.

This paragraph focuses on the wider record of the Federal Government. This balances the previous paragraph, which focused only on the achievements of the Federal Government.

However, the federal government was not always helpful in the fight for civil rights. After the Brown and Brown II decisions, President Eisenhower refused to publically welcome the rulings. Kennedy was also concerned that black campaigners wanted too much, too soon. After the Freedom Rides, he called for a period of 'cooling off', effectively asking for a halt to the campaign for black rights. Rather, in 1962, he set up the Voter Education Project to try to persuade black activists to abandon direct action in favour of voter registration. Even Johnson refused to work with King following King's criticism of America's war in Vietnam. Johnson's final civil rights Act, the Fair Housing Act of 1968, was also largely ineffective because Congress refused to allow the Government the power to enforce it. What is more, for much of the period 1955 to 1968, Congress hindered the advancement of civil rights. Congress changed the 1957 Civil Rights Act, reducing the penalties for stopping black people registering to vote. Equally, in 1960, Senators filibustered for 83 days to try to stop the Civil Rights Act of that year. Evidently, for much of the period the Federal Government was of little help, because the presidents were not willing to endorse the campaigns of black activists and because Congress tried to undermine important legislation.

The most important reason for the advancement of civil rights was the campaigns of black activists. The Montgomery Bus Boycott brought together a grass roots campaign and a legal campaign to force *de jure* desegregation of the buses in Montgomery. The Little Rock campaign forced President Eisenhower to take control of the National Guard and help black students enrol at a white school. The Freedom Rides of 1961 forced the President to intervene and desegregate interstate transport and transport facilities. Finally, in 1963, the Birmingham campaign and the March on Washington maintained pressure on the President to draw up a Civil Rights Bill. The actions of black protesters were the most significant reason for the advancement of civil rights because they forced the Federal Government to take its responsibility seriously and use its power to address segregation and disenfranchisement.

The media also played an important role in the advancement of civil rights. Indeed, without media attention, the campaigns of black activists may not have had such a significant impact. For example, the Birmingham campaign of 1963 attracted media attention all over the world. Indeed, the Soviet Union devoted one-fifth of its news coverage to the protest, showing local police using water cannon and dogs on young protestors. In the context of the Cold War, this was an important propaganda victory for the Soviet Union. In addition, the March on Washington of the same year attracted a great deal of positive media coverage and forced Kennedy to begin work on the 1964 Civil Rights Act. In this way, the campaigns of black activists highlighted the extent of racism in America, but media coverage of the campaigns ensured that the Federal Government took steps to address this racism.

The Federal Government played an important role in the advancement of civil rights, particularly in the period 1964 to 1965. However, for much of the period the Federal Government was unwilling to use its power to end racism. Essentially, the campaigns of civil rights groups such as the NAACP, SCLC, CORE and SNCC, coupled with media coverage of these campaigns, forced the Government to do the right thing.

This paragraph also addresses the question, but shifts the focus from the stated factor to the issue of black protest. In this sense, it extends the scope of the essay. It also examines the way in which black protest put pressure on the Federal Government, and therefore begins to create an overall argument.

Here, the candidate builds on the previous paragraphs by showing the way that the media interacted with black protest and government action. Again, the candidate is developing an overall argument throughout the essay.

The conclusion produces a focused summary, which recaps the main points and underlines the argument that has run throughout the essay.

30/30

This essay considers a range of factors that contributed to the advancement of civil rights in the period 1955–68. Each factor is dealt with in considerable detail, and the answer also makes an argument that the protests of black people, coupled with media attention, was the most significant factor in bringing about this change. Due to the sustained analysis, and the range and depth of the supporting evidence, this essay achieves a mark at the top of Level 5.

Two types of question

Exam-style questions can take two forms.

- Questions that require you to consider a range of factors – either causes or consequences.
- Questions that require you to make a judgement about the impact of a single factor.

Answers to the first type of question need to consider a range of factors. Answers to the second type of question need to consider different aspects of a single factor.

The essay above answers the first type of question, and consequently addresses a range of factors that advanced civil rights in the period 1955–68. The following question is on the same topic, but is a single factor question. Draw a plan for your answer to this question.

How successful was the Federal Government in advancing civil rights in the period 1955–68?

Section 3:
Black Power and the use of violence

Malcolm X

Peaceful protest was not as attractive to black Americans in the Northern states. **Black Nationalism** and **Black Power** were popular alternatives to King's philosophy.

Early life and the Nation of Islam

Malcolm X's early life was dogged by tragedy: his father was murdered by **white supremacists** and his mother had a nervous breakdown. In his teens, he moved to Boston, where he became involved in crime. He was imprisoned and while in jail he converted to the Nation of Islam.

Nation of Islam

Founded in 1930, the Nation of Islam taught that **Allah** created black people. White people were created by an evil scientist called Yacub, making them incapable of goodness.

The Nation of Islam argued in favour of **Black separatism**. They argued that black people could only be free in an environment where there were no white people.

Criticisms of King

Malcolm X criticised Martin Luther King for three reasons.

First, Malcolm X accused King of pandering to powerful white people. He argued that the March on Washington was organised by 'a bunch of **Uncle Toms**' who were really serving their white masters.

Secondly, Malcolm X criticised King's emphasis on peace. He argued that it was unnatural to allow your enemy to abuse you without fighting back. Moreover, self-defence was entirely legal, as was gun ownership, and therefore Malcolm X advocated both. He argued that white people would only take black people seriously if they stood up for themselves.

Thirdly, King argued that racial integration was a 'dream'. Malcolm X described it as a 'nightmare'. Essentially, Malcolm X believed that an integrated society would simply lead to new forms of slavery. Black people, he argued, would form the **underclass** in an integrated society, acting as **pimps**, drug dealers and prostitutes.

Black Nationalism

Malcolm X described himself as a 'Black Nationalist freedom fighter'. By Black Nationalism, he meant two things.

- Political Black Nationalism – black people should govern themselves.
- Economic Black Nationalism – black people should control the economy within their communities.

Black Nationalism was extremely popular in the black **ghettos** of the North because it asserted black independence and dignity.

Organisation of Afro-American Unity (OAAU)

In 1964, Malcolm X left the Nation of Islam. His relationship with the leader, **Elijah Muhammad**, had become difficult due to Muhammad's jealousy of Malcolm X, and Malcolm X's discovery that his leader was having affairs.

Malcolm X rethought his position and formed the **OAAU** as a political organisation that would collaborate with other **civil rights groups** to campaign for better housing and education. Towards the end of his life, he even started talking about working with sympathetic white people.

Malcolm X's assassination

Malcolm X was assassinated in February 1965. He was shot fifteen times at close range. The three men convicted of his murder were all members of the Nation of Islam.

Complete the paragraph

Below are a sample exam-style question and a paragraph written in answer to this question. The paragraph contains a point and specific examples, but lacks a concluding explanatory link back to the question. Complete the paragraph adding this link in the space provided.

Why did black protest become more radical during the 1960s?

One reason why black protest became more radical during the 1960s was the influence of Malcolm X. Malcolm X put forward a series of very convincing criticisms of Martin Luther King. First, he argued that Martin Luther King was an 'Uncle Tom', by which he meant he slavishly obeyed his white masters. Secondly, he criticised Martin Luther King's pacifism, arguing that it was natural to want to defend yourself and your community. Finally, he argued that Martin Luther King's dream was in fact a nightmare, as integration would lead to a new kind of slavery for black people.

_____

_____

_____

Eliminate irrelevance

Below are a sample exam-style question and a paragraph written in answer to this question. Read the paragraph and identify parts that are not directly relevant to the question. Draw a line through the information that is irrelevant and justify your deletions in the margin.

Why was the civil rights movement increasingly divided during the 1960s?

One of the reasons why the civil rights movement was increasingly divided during the 1960s was the influence of Malcolm X and the Nation of Islam. Malcolm X had a tragic early life due to the murder of his father and his mother's nervous breakdown. He argued in favour of 'Black Nationalism'. By this he meant that black people should govern themselves rather than being controlled by white politicians and that black people should be self-sufficient through community control of the economies within the ghettos. This message was extremely popular among the black working class in the Northern states because, unlike Martin Luther King's message, it addressed the social and economic problems of the Northern ghettos. Also, the Nation of Islam taught that white people were created by a white scientist named Yacub. In this way, the civil rights movement became increasingly divided because Malcolm X offered an attractive alternative to the campaign for integration.

The radicalisation of SNCC and CORE

Revised

During the 1960s, **radicals** in the **civil rights movement** became critical of the philosophy and methods of King. By the late 1960s, **SNCC** and **CORE** had embraced a new philosophy – Black Power.

Criticisms of King

King's willingness to work with white politicians, his decision to postpone the Selma march in order to appease Johnson, and the failure of his Chicago campaign led to criticism. By the mid-1960s, radicals within SNCC and CORE felt that King's approach was not assertive enough and was reinforcing the stereotype that black people were passive and needed the help of white people to achieve their goals.

The Meredith March

In 1962, **James Meredith** was the first black student to enrol at the University of Mississippi. In 1966, Meredith staged a one-man march to celebrate his achievement – the March Against Fear. During the march, he was shot and wounded by a white racist, and as a result the **SCLC** and SNCC continued the march on his behalf.

Stokely Carmichael, the leader of SNCC, argued that Meredith's shooting necessitated a change in strategy. White people, he argued, were prepared to use violence against unarmed black people, and therefore the time had come to embrace self-defence. Carmichael's new slogan was 'Black Power'.

Black Power

From 1966, SNCC and CORE embraced Black Power. For Carmichael, this meant that black people should direct their own struggle for freedom, independent of white help. Consequently, SNCC expelled its white members in 1966, and CORE did the same in 1968.

Black Power focused on issues of integration, community control and black culture.

Carmichael argued that black people should seek integration from a point of strength. He argued that King had been prepared to settle for integration as second-class **citizens**. In contrast, Carmichael argued that integration should be carried out on the terms set by black people.

Carmichael also argued that the civil rights movement had become obsessed with integration. Rather than integration, Carmichael argued that black people needed to fight for better educational and housing facilities. Improving the conditions of black people was the primary goal. He argued that this was best achieved by black people controlling the schools and housing associations in their communities, rather than through seeking integration.

Traditionally, Carmichael argued, integration had been based on the idea that there was nothing of value in black culture, and that black people had a lot to learn from the white community. Carmichael argued that this conception of integration was racist. Similarly, he argued that black leaders needed to speak the language of the ghettos, and dress as Africans, rather than putting on suits and speaking like white politicians.

Collaboration with King

The radicalisation of SNCC and CORE made continuing collaboration with the **NAACP** impossible. During 1966, King and SCLC continued to collaborate with SNCC and CORE. However, from the end of 1966, SNCC and CORE were not prepared to collaborate with SCLC. Divisions within the black rights movement severely weakened its effectiveness.

Identify an argument

a

Below are a series of definitions, a sample exam-style question and two sample conclusions. One of the conclusions achieves a high level because it contains an argument. The other achieves a lower level because it contains only description and assertion. Identify which is which. The mark scheme on page 3 will help you.

- **Description:** a detailed account.
- **Assertion:** a statement of fact or an opinion that is not supported by a reason.
- **Reason:** a statement that explains or justifies something.
- **Argument:** an assertion justified with a reason.

How accurate is it to say that the main characteristic of Black Power was its advocacy of violence?

Sample 1

Black Power was about much more than violence because Black Power was critical of a great deal in the traditional civil rights movement. Obviously, Black Power radicals did argue in favour of self-defence, and even advocated gun ownership in the black community. However, Black Power was also about a great deal more, such as community control of housing and education, and celebrating black culture. The most important aspect of Black Power was its criticism of integration as it had been traditionally understood because it changed the strategy of SNCC and CORE away from fighting segregation towards fighting for better social and economic conditions.

Sample 2

Black Power was about a number of different issues. Following the Meredith March, Stokely Carmichael argued that the time had come to abandon peaceful protest. Black Power also advocated a different kind of integration because Black Power radicals were concerned that integration might leave black people as second-class citizens. Finally, Black Power was critical of Martin Luther King for his willingness to work with white politicians. Overall, Black Power was about a number of different issues.

Turning assertion into argument

a

Below are a sample exam-style question and a series of assertions. Read the question and then add a justification to each of the assertions to turn it into an argument.

Why did the Black Power movement emerge during the 1960s?

The shooting of James Meredith contributed to the emergence of Black Power because

_____

_____

The influence of Malcolm X was a key reason for the emergence of Black Power because

_____

_____

Criticisms of Martin Luther King led to the emergence of Black Power because

_____

_____

The Black Panthers

Revised

The Black Panther Party for Self-Defence was formed in Oakland, California in 1966. Huey P. Newton and Bobby Seale, the founders, argued that the group was formed 'in the spirit of Malcolm X'. The Panthers became the best-known advocates of Black Power.

'Patrol the Pigs'

The Panther's first concern was to counter police brutality, which was a constant feature of life in the Northern ghettos. Consequently, the Panthers set up street patrols – pairs of armed Panthers dressed in black leather jackets, dark glasses and berets would keep the police under surveillance. The programme demonstrated their commitment to **communal self-defence**. Newton spearheaded the campaign, patrolling Oakland in his car. Newton knew the law, and used this knowledge to hold the police to account.

The California state authorities tried to stamp out the Panthers' patrols. The police used a variety of methods against the Panthers.

- They engaged Panthers in gun battles. On one occasion, a squad of 50 armed police were sent to arrest two well-known Panthers. The police opened fire, killing Lil' Bobby Hutton, a teenager, and one of the first to join the Panthers.
- They arrested leading members of the Panthers. Huey Newton was arrested on murder charges in 1967. However, the charges were dropped and he was released in 1970.

Survival programmes

Following Newton's arrest, the Panthers took a new direction. From 1968 the Panthers ran a series of welfare programmes, which reflected their commitment to **community self-help**.

Programme	Effectiveness
Free breakfasts for schoolchildren	• By 1969 the programme was feeding 10,000 black children every day.
Free health clinics	• By 1974 there were 200 free clinics across the USA, treating 200,000 people a year. • The campaign highlighted the need for investment in treatments for **sickle cell anaemia**.
Liberation Schools	• Literacy and numeracy classes helped schoolchildren who were struggling in mainstream education, as well as adults who had little formal education. • Black history classes inspired self-respect and black pride through focusing on the achievement of black historical figures.

The popularity of the Panthers

The Panthers were genuinely popular in the Northern ghettos.

- By 1968 the Black Panthers' newspaper had a circulation of 250,000, and a readership of one million.
- Leading Panthers, including Newton and Seale, had a 70 per cent approval rating among black **GIs** serving in Vietnam.

COINTELPRO

The **FBI** attempted to undermine the Black Panthers. COINTELPRO engaged in a campaign of dirty tricks against the party. This included phone-tapping, audio surveillance of the homes and offices of leading members of the Panthers, and even forging letters supposedly from the Black Panthers to show that they were plotting to assassinate senior members of the Government.

Simple essay style

Below is a sample exam-style question. Use your own knowledge and the information on the opposite page to produce a plan for an answer to this question. Choose four general points, and provide three pieces of specific information to support each point. Once you have planned your essay, write the introduction and conclusion for the essay. The introduction should list the points to be discussed in the essay. The conclusion should summarise the key points and justify which point was the most important.

'The use of violence was a significant feature of the Black Power movement.' How far do you agree with this statement?

You're the examiner

Below are a sample exam-style question and a paragraph written in answer to this question. Read the paragraph and the mark scheme provided on page 3. Decide which level you would award the paragraph. Write the level below, along with a justification for your choice.

How far did Black Power groups address the social and economic problems that faced black Americans in the 1960s?

There were lots of social and economic problems that faced black people in America. In the Second World War there was a great migration from the South to the North. This helped black people because they earned higher wages in the North than they did in the South. One Black Power group tried to help by policing the pigs, but this led to gun battles and didn't help very much. This was in the Northern states not the Southern states. Black Power groups did address the problems of black people.

Level: Reason for choosing this level:

_____

_____

SNCC, 1966–68

Between 1966 and 1968, SNCC embarked on a series of campaigns to improve the living and working conditions of black citizens across America. In this sense, SNCC was attempting to put Black Power into practice.

Freedom Cities

SNCC attempted to empower black communities by setting up 'Freedom Cities'; cities where black people were involved in electing **school boards** and police chiefs. They believed that by involving black people in running the services that affected their lives, they would be able to improve those services and therefore improve their lives.

The 'Free D.C.' Movement, 1966–68

Marion Barry, a senior member of SNCC based in Washington D.C., pioneered the 'Freedom City' initiative in America's capital. Starting in 1966, SNCC organised mass demonstrations, demanding the **democratisation** of local school boards. By the end of the year, all citizens had the right to participate in elections to choose the members of school boards. In this way, black parents gained control over the schools in their communities and therefore were able to influence the curriculum and methods of teaching.

Barry was also involved in creating a 'model police precinct', which, like the school boards, was elected by the local community. SNCC lobbied the Government and gained $3 million of funding to improve community policing through better training.

Mississippi Freedom City, 1966–67

SNCC, working with local churches, attempted to set up a similar programme in Mississippi. SNCC, the churches and **federal government** raised $1.5 million in order to set up 85 Head Start centres to support young children. Head Start centres focused on providing childcare and educational resources to children of poor families, the majority of whom were black.

The project was opposed by Ross R. Barnett, the State Governor, and John C. Stennis, the local Senator. This political opposition led to the closure of the project in 1967, but not before it had improved the lives of thousands of black children.

Black culture

SNCC argued that white people assumed that there was nothing of value in the black community. In the late 1960s, they sought to challenge this.

Carmichael, for example, adopted a new African name, Kwame Ture, emphasising his African culture and African roots. He took the name out of respect for the Ghanaian revolutionary, **Kwame Nkrumah**.

Similarly, **Angela Davis** became famous for her Afro hairstyle. In the 1950s and early 1960s, black people had often tried to straighten their hair in order to fit in with white styles. In the late 1960s, the Afro hairstyle became a symbol that people were embracing their black identity and recognising that black was beautiful.

The most important achievement of this period was the change in language brought about by Black Power. The words 'negro' and 'coloured' fell out of use and were replaced with the word 'black'. This was important because black people were rejecting words associated with segregation and slavery, and asserting a new, independent identity.

Below are a sample exam-style question and a timeline. Read the question, study the timeline and, using three coloured pens, put a red, amber or green star next to the events to show:

- red – events and policies that have no relevance to the question
- amber – events and policies that have some significance to the question
- green – events and policies that are directly relevant to the question.

1. **How accurate is it to say that Black Power achieved nothing for black Americans?**

			Malcolm X assassinated		Memphis sanitation workers' strike
		Malcolm X leaves the Nation of Islam and forms the Organisation of Afro-American Unity (OAAU)	Selma campaign	Freedom Cities movement begins	Martin Luther King assassinated
			President Johnson increases American involvement in Vietnam	March Against Fear	
Greensboro sit-ins	Freedom Rides	Birmingham campaign		Chicago campaign	Civil Rights Act
1960	**1961**	**1963**	**1964**	**1965**	**1966**	**1968**
Student Non-violent Co-ordination Committee founded (SNCC)	Albany campaign begins	March on Washington	Mississippi Freedom Summer	Publication of the Moynihan Report	Black Panthers founded	Poor People's campaign
			Civil Rights Act	Voting Rights Act	SNCC expels white members	CORE expels white members

Now repeat the activity with the following questions. You could use different colours, or number your stars 1, 2 or 3.

2. **Why did more militant forms of protest emerge in the 1960s?**

3. **How accurate is it to say that as the black rights movement became more divided, it achieved less?**

Below are a sample exam-style question and a list of general points that could be used to answer the question. Use your own knowledge and the information on the opposite page to reach a judgement about the importance of these points to the question posed. Write numbers on the spectrum below to indicate their relative importance. Then write a brief justification of your placement, explaining why some of these factors are more important than others. The resulting diagram could form the basis of an essay plan.

How important were divisions amongst civil rights activists in explaining the failure of the civil rights movement in the late 1960s?

1. Divisions among civil rights activists
2. The Black Power movement
3. The Vietnam War
4. The expense of further reform
5. Martin Luther King's Northern campaigns
6. Alienation of white liberals

Very important ←——————————————————————→ Less important

The achievements of Black Power

Revised

Black Power groups are often criticised for not achieving substantial legal change. This, however, was not their goal. Black Power attempted to bring about cultural, social and economic change, and in these areas it undoubtedly succeeded.

Cultural change

In the late 1960s, culture changed, influenced by Black Power. There was greater emphasis on strong black role models and the importance of African culture.

Aspect of culture	Achievements
Music	• In 1965, **Miles Davis** forced his record company to replace an image of a white woman with an image of a black woman on the cover of his album, *ESP*. • In 1968, Miles Davis released *Bitches Brew*, heavily influenced by African musical styles and with a cover image based on African art. • In 1968, Miles Davis reformed his band, excluding all white members.
Television	• In 1966, the television series *Star Trek* was launched. It included a black character, Lieutenant Uhura, played by Nichelle Nichols. Uhura was highly educated and technically skilled. Her name was derived from the **Swahili** word for freedom. • In 1966, *Star Trek* featured the first inter-racial kiss on colour television. • In 1968, a black actress, Eartha Kitt, was cast as Catwoman in the television series *Batman*.
Sport	• At the 1968 Mexico City Olympics, two black American athletes gave the **Black Power salute** during the medal ceremony for the 200 m sprint.

Social and economic change

The Black Panthers and groups such as SNCC and CORE ran campaigns to improve the health and education of America's black citizens.

Type of change	Achievements
Health	• The Black Panthers set up 200 free health clinics, treating 200,000 people a year. • The clinics encouraged investment in research to tackle sickle cell anaemia. • In 1972, the Government passed the National Sickle Cell Anaemia Control Act, granting government money for research and treatment.
Education	• The Black Panthers' Free Breakfasts for Schoolchildren programme fed 10,000 black children every day. • The Liberation Schools increased literacy and numeracy skills among black students, and encouraged the study of black history. • SNCC's Mississippi Freedom City set up 85 Head Start centres to support young children. • SNCC's Freedom D.C. movement won parents the right to elect their school boards.

Conclusion

Black Power is often remembered for its emphasis on self-defence, in contrast to King's methods of peaceful protest. However, Black Power was about much more than self-defence. It also included a commitment to bring about cultural change and to improve the social and economic conditions for black people across America.

Spectrum of significance

Below is a sample exam question and a list of general points which could be used to answer the question. Use your own knowledge and the information on the opposite page to reach a judgement about the importance of these general points to the question posed. Write numbers on the spectrum below to indicate their relative importance. Having done this, write a brief justification of your placement, explaining why some of these factors are more important than others. The resulting diagram could form the basis of an essay plan.

How far do you agree that Black Power made a significant difference to the position of black Americans during the 1960s?

1. Cultural change
2. Social change
3. Economic change

←——→

Very significant   Less significant

Complex essay style

Below are a sample exam-style question, a list of key points to be made in the essay, and a simple introduction and conclusion for the essay. Read the question, the key points and the introduction and conclusion. Rewrite the introduction and the conclusion in order to develop an argument.

How far do you agree that Black Power made a significant difference to the position of black Americans during the 1960s?

Key points
- Cultural change
- Social change
- Economic change

Introduction

There were three main ways in which Black Power made a difference to the lives of black Americans. It made a difference to culture, black society, and the economic position of black Americans.

Conclusion

There were three main ways in which Black Power made a difference to the lives of black Americans. The most important was cultural change because it had the most impact.

Recommended reading

Below is a list of suggested further reading on this topic.

- Gary Gerstle, *American Crucible: Race and Nation in the Twentieth Century* (Princeton University Press, 2002), pages 295–310.
- Simon Hall, *Peace and Freedom: The Civil Rights and Antiwar Movements in the 1960s* (University of Pennsylvania Press, 2006), pages 1–12.
- Charles Earl Jones, *The Black Panther Party (Reconsidered)* (Black Classic Press, 1998), pages 1–21.

Exam focus

Revised

Below is a sample A-grade essay. Read the essay and the examiner's comments around it.

Why did the fight for black rights become increasingly militant in the years 1960 to 1968?

The introduction sets up a range of factors that explain the increase in militancy in this period.

The fight for black rights became increasingly militant during the 1960s for a number of reasons. These included the influence of Malcolm X, the failures of Martin Luther King, the experience of the March Against Fear and finally, the nature of the problems of the North.

Malcolm X was a leading member of the Nation of Islam until 1964. He was critical of peaceful protest for a number of reasons. Essentially, he accused King of being a modern-day 'Uncle Tom' — that is to say, a black man who was happy to be manipulated by white people. Malcolm X believed that King was an 'Uncle Tom' as King refused to use self-defence. King turned the other cheek when confronted by white violence. He even refused to fight back when black people were killed. As a result, Malcolm X argued that King made black people look weak. Malcolm X also said that King's dream was a nightmare. Integration, according to Malcolm X, would lead to a society in which black people were forced to take the worst jobs and forced to turn to prostitution and drug dealing by white people who wanted to exploit them. His alternative was Black Nationalism, by which he meant that black people should control the politics of their neighbourhoods and be economically self-sufficient. Malcolm X's influence led to greater militancy in the fight for black rights because he made a strong case for rejecting peaceful protest, and advocated Black Nationalism rather than integration.

This paragraph explains a range of ways in which Malcolm X's influence led to radicalisation in the movement as a whole.

King's failures also led to increasing militancy. For example, during the Selma campaign of 1965, King agreed to postpone the march at the request of President Johnson. The Albany campaign of 1961–62 was also a failure. Local police chief Laurie Pritchett instructed the police to treat black protestors with respect. As a result, there was no violence, no media attention and therefore no pressure for change. The campaign showed that violence was an important part of the campaign's success. Clearly, King's failures helped to increase militancy because they made King and his method look ineffective and therefore black people looked for an alternative.

Here, the candidate gives an overview of King's campaigns from 1961–65, covering a range of different examples.

James Meredith's March Against Fear of 1966 was a turning point in the movement. Meredith had been the first black student at the University of Mississippi. In 1966 he started a march across the South. Sadly, he was shot and wounded early on in the march and was unable to complete his campaign. SNCC, CORE and SCLC stepped in to complete the march. However, Carmichael argued that the shooting

Having given an overview of King's campaigns, this paragraph discusses one campaign in detail. Evidently, the candidate can employ both range and depth of knowledge.

of Meredith showed that it was time for black people to defend themselves and abandon peaceful protest. Marchers from SNCC and CORE adopted the slogan 'Black Power' during the march, to show that they were no longer committed to King's pacifist methods. Militancy increased following the March Against Fear because many black activists agreed with Carmichael that increasing white violence meant that the time for peaceful protest was over.

Finally, the fight for black rights became increasingly militant because the problems of the North were very different to the problems of the South. King's Chicago campaign had attempted to address the problems of bad housing and poverty in the ghettos. Sadly, peaceful protest was less effective at dealing with these problems than it had been at dealing with the problems of segregation and disenfranchisement in the South. The Black Panther Party for Self-Defense, founded in Oakland, California in 1966, was much more militant and also much more successful at dealing with the problems of the North. Its first campaign, Patrol the Pigs, effectively confronted police brutality by ensuring that armed Panthers who knew the law kept the police under surveillance. Equally, its Survival Programmes of 1968 effectively confronted the problems of poverty in the ghettos. The Free Breakfasts for Schoolchildren programme fed 10,000 black children every day during 1969, and its free clinic programme provided effective screening for sickle cell anaemia, a health problem predominantly affecting black people. In this way, the problems of the North led to increased militancy as they highlighted the limitations of King's moderate campaigns and the effectiveness of the more militant approach of groups like the Black Panthers.

Overall, there were several related reasons for the increasing militancy of the fight for black rights from 1960 to 1968. Malcolm X's criticisms of King became increasingly influential as King's campaigns in the North ran into difficulty in the late 1960s. At the same time, Black Nationalism and Black Power became more attractive due to increasing white violence and as an effective alternative to King's methods in the ghettos of the North.

This paragraph addresses the Black Panthers' campaigns in 1968 and therefore the essay covers the entire period set in the question.

The conclusion provides a focused summary of the argument.

24/30

This essay considers a range of factors that explain why the struggle for black rights became more militant in the years 1960–68. It does not enter Level 5 because it does not relate the different factors to each other. Nonetheless, a good level of detail ensures that this essay gets the top mark in Level 4.

Moving from Level 4 to Level 5

The exam focus at the end of Section 1 (pages 14–15) provided a Level 5 essay. The essay here achieves a Level 4. Read both essays, and the examiner's comments provided. Make a list of the additional features required to push a Level 4 essay into Level 5.

Section 4:
The changing economic and social environment of the 1960s

Mass culture

Revised

During the 1960s, American culture changed radically. The independent and **individualistic** culture, which had characterised America for centuries, gave way to a mass culture, in which people worked for big corporations, bought the same products, watched the same television, and read the same newspapers.

Corporate culture

One aspect of American mass culture was the rise in large corporations. By the end of the Second World War, 70 per cent of American manufacturing was produced by just 100 companies, each employing tens of thousands of people. This led to the emergence of a new corporate culture, which stressed conformity and working hard to please the boss, rather than independence.

Nonetheless, this loss of independence went hand in hand with higher wages. By 1960, 62 per cent of homes were owner-occupied, compared with 44 per cent in 1940. There was also a consumer boom in the 1960s. By 1970, half of the adult population owned cars. America's new-found wealth fuelled a new mass media. By 1960, 90 per cent of American households owned a television.

Mainstream politics

The 1960s was a decade of political change. Americans who had lived through the **Great Depression** were afraid of poverty and therefore voted for political parties that they trusted to keep the economy growing and taxes low.

The new generation, who started voting in the 1960s, had never experienced poverty, and therefore had different political priorities. Consequently, young people voting in the 1960s were attracted by **political idealism**.

Kennedy's New Frontier

President Kennedy appealed to young voters because of his idealism and youth. He was committed to a new politics, which he described as the 'New Frontier'. He had two ambitious projects:

- the space program – Kennedy promised to land a man on the moon by the end of the decade
- the Peace Corps – sending 15,000 volunteers to work overseas in developing nations.

Johnson's Great Society

President Johnson was committed to tackling poverty, and in so doing, making America a 'Great Society'. In his first two years in office, he worked with **Congress** to pass 435 **bills**, committing $3.4 billion to regenerate America's inner cities and improve schools.

The failure of mainstream politics

Neither the New Frontier, nor the Great Society, succeeded in addressing America's deep-seated social problems. Moreover, Johnson committed America to fight communism in Vietnam, and in so doing, diverted vast resources away from social reform. Consequently, young idealists turned away from mainstream politics during the 1960s, looking for more radical alternatives.

Rejecting conformity

During the 1960s, American mass culture was dominated by a new corporate culture, a mass culture, and a mainstream politics that failed to deliver a fairer society. The lack of individualism in modern America frustrated many young people who wanted a better society in which people were genuinely free to be themselves. Conservatives described this as the 'cult of individual freedom'.

Use the information on the opposite page to add detail to the mind map below.

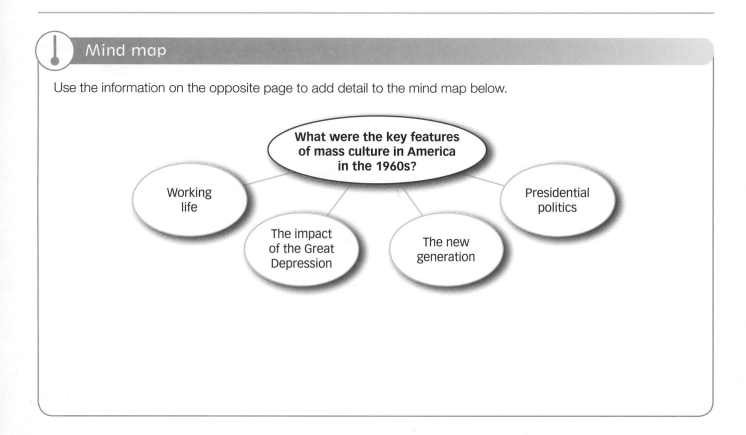

Below are a sample exam-style question and a paragraph written in answer to this question. Read the paragraph and identify parts that are not directly relevant to the question. Draw a line through the information that is irrelevant and justify your deletions in the margin.

How accurate is it to say that American society was dominated by a cult of individual freedom in the years 1960–68?

In lots of ways American society was not dominated by the cult of individual freedom. At work, more and more people were working for big businesses with a corporate culture that demanded conformity. In big corporations, the emphasis was on impressing your boss rather than standing out as an individual. Corporations produced a great deal of money, which financed impressive projects that formed part of Kennedy's 'New Frontier'. The most impressive was the space program, which Kennedy had committed to landing a man on the moon. Equally, leisure time was dominated by the mass media, particularly television programmes. In fact, by 1960, 90 per cent of Americans lived in a household with a television. Martin Luther King and other civil rights leaders used this new medium to get their message about black rights across to the whole of America. The consumer boom of the 1960s also meant that more and more people were buying the same kinds of products. In this way, there were large aspects of American life where individualism seemed to be under attack.

Counterculture and the anti-war movement

The mainstream culture of the 1960s provoked a rebellion in large sections of America's youth.

Teen culture

By the early 1960s, American teenagers were spending $10 million a year. Big business was keen to capitalise on this market with films, music and fashion.

Elvis Presley was the teen idol of America's rock 'n' roll scene. He horrified the older generation, who described him as a 'sexhibitionist' on account of his provocative dancing.

In film, too, glamorous outsiders attracted young people while horrifying their parents. **James Dean**, star of the film *Rebel without a Cause* (1955), explicitly rejected the established authority of parents and schools.

The 1960s gave birth to a new generation who were more critical of authority and more willing to experiment with sex, drugs and rock 'n' roll.

Counterculture

The American counterculture comprised a variety of movements that rejected the values and style of mainstream culture.

Beatniks and hippies

The beatniks, or 'Beat Generation', emerged in the late 1950s. Rather than consumer culture, the beatniks were interested in drugs, sex, philosophy and poetry. They rejected gender stereotypes. Male beatniks grew their hair long, while female beatniks wore their hair short. **William S. Burroughs'** book, *Naked Lunch* (1959), was an important influence. It described a trip across America under the influence of hallucinogenic drugs.

The hippies, or 'Flower Children', emerged in the mid-1960s. The Diggers in San Francisco, to take one example, set up an anarchist commune in 1966.

The commune's members enjoyed free healthcare, free transport, free food, free drugs and free love. Hippies tended to have long hair and wear clothes made from natural fabrics.

The mainstream press were horrified by the beatniks and the hippies, branding them as 'un-American'.

Anti-war protest

The anti-war movement started in America's universities. Students for a Democratic Society (SDS) believed that American society had ceased to be truly **democratic**. SDS argued that an end to **capitalism** would bring about true human freedom.

SDS remained a small movement until America's involvement in the **Vietnam War**. In April 1965, SDS organised an anti-war rally in Washington D.C., attracting over 20,000 people. SDS also organised '**teach-ins**' at universities and a second anti-war march to Washington in November 1965, which attracted 40,000 people. The Diggers also organised an anti-war protest – a 'human be-in'. This was a free pop concert attracting 30,000 people.

Burning **draft cards** was another form of anti-war protest. The Government criminalised the burning of draft cards, but young people continued to symbolically reject the war in this way.

The impact of the anti-war movement

As a result of the anti-war campaign membership of the SDS increased from 1,500 in 1965 to 30,000 by 1967. However, by 1968, only 28 per cent of people actively opposed the war. Moreover, the protests had little impact on government policy. President Johnson continued to despatch troops to Vietnam. Finally, the media broadly supported the war, editing its footage. Between 1965 and 1970, only 76 of the 2,300 news reports from Vietnam showed images of dead or wounded soldiers.

Simple essay style

Below are two sample exam-style questions. Use your own knowledge and the information on the opposite page to produce plans for answers to these questions. For each essay, choose four general points, and provide three pieces of specific information to support each point. Once you have planned each essay, write the introduction and conclusion. The introduction should list the points to be discussed in the essay. The conclusion should summarise the key points and justify which point was the most important.

1. How accurate is it to say that American culture was dominated by protest in the years 1960–68?

2. How far did American youth culture aim to challenge political power in America in the period 1960–68?

Develop the detail

a

Below are a sample exam-style question and a paragraph written in answer to this question. The paragraph contains a limited amount of detail. Annotate the paragraph to add additional detail to the answer.

How successful was the American protest culture of the 1960s?

Counterculture in the 1960s was very successful. For example, the student movement grew in popularity after the outbreak of the Vietnam War, staging a number of protests. In addition, the hippy movement was very popular among young people and a number of notable communes were formed. The drug culture also played a significant role in the success of the movement. Writers and artists formed part of this movement, publishing works that challenged accepted traditions. In this way, the counterculture movement of the 1960s succeeded in gaining the support of many young people, spreading its anti-war message and its countercultural values through literature and drugs.

Feminism

Revised

During the 1960s, women campaigned for greater economic and social rights. Towards the end of the 1960s, more radical feminists were also challenging stereotypes of what it meant to be a woman and seeking new ways of relating to each other and to men.

Second wave feminism

Second wave feminism addressed economic and social issues. In the 1960s, three-fifths of women over the age of sixteen had no paid employment. Moreover, working women earned 57 per cent of the average male working wage.

Feminists identified a series of problems in terms of women's economic position.

- Women were responsible for 79 per cent of America's unpaid domestic work.
- Working women were expected to work a double shift: formal employment and housework.
- Men got paid more than women for doing the same job.

Informal pressure

Feminists put pressure on the Kennedy Government to bring about change. This led to the creation of the Presidential Commission on the Status of Women. This commission succeeded in gaining the addition of a clause in the 1964 Civil Rights Act, outlawing sexual discrimination in the workplace. However, the Government refused to enforce this section of the Civil Rights Act, and therefore discrimination continued.

Legal campaigns

The National Organisation for Women (NOW), founded by **Betty Friedan**, pursued a number of **court cases** based on the Civil Rights Act.

Third wave feminism

Radical feminists split from NOW in 1968 over the issue of lesbianism. NOW was unwilling to champion lesbian rights for fear of losing the support of men. **Third wave feminism** was concerned with the issue of identity. These feminists believed that men treated women as sex objects, and that women should abandon relationships with men in favour of celibacy or lesbianism. For example, Kate Millet left NOW and set up The Feminists. The Feminists campaigned against pornography and marriage, and in favour of abortion, which at the time was illegal.

A similar group, the New York Radical Women (NYRW), organised 'Speak Outs' in which women would openly discuss the experience of having abortions. NYRW also held a protest against the 1968 Miss America pageant, in which they crowned a sheep Miss America.

Roe v. Wade

During the 1960s, feminists were unable to force the legalisation of abortion. A traditional legal campaign, *Roe v. Wade*, finally succeeded in relaxing America's abortion laws in 1973.

Date	Case	Outcome
1968	*Commonwealth of Pennsylvania v. Daniel*	• Jane Daniel was convicted of robbery and given a much longer sentence than her male accomplice. • Daniel won the case and her sentence was reduced. The Muncy Act, which stated that women should receive longer sentences than men, was struck down.
1969	*Weeks v. Southern Bell*	• Lorena Weeks claimed that Southern Bell had discriminated against her by promoting a man above her even though she had more experience. • Weeks won $31,000 in back pay and a promotion.

Below are a sample exam-style question and a paragraph written in answer to this question. Read the paragraph and decide which of the possible options (in bold) is most appropriate. Delete the least appropriate options and complete the paragraph by justifying your selection.

How far did the Civil Rights Act of 1964 end discrimination across America?

The Civil Rights Act had a **great/fair/limited** impact on sexual discrimination in America. The Act contained a clause that outlawed discrimination against women in the workplace. However, this *de jure* victory did not immediately lead to *de facto* change. In fact, the Government refused to devote any resources to enforcing the clause of the Act that outlawed sexual discrimination. Nonetheless, the National Organisation of Women (NOW) supported court cases that forced the Government and private companies to recognise the rights of women. For example, the 1968 case *Commonwealth of Pennsylvania v. Daniel* overturned the Muncy Act, an Act that meant female criminals were automatically given longer sentences than male prisoners who had committed the same crime. Clearly, the Civil Rights Act had a **great/fair/limited** impact on discrimination against women because

_____

_____

_____

Below are a sample exam-style question, a list of key points to be made in the essay, and a simple introduction and conclusion for the essay. Read the question, the key points and the introduction and conclusion. Rewrite the introduction and the conclusion in order to develop an argument.

How successful was the campaign for women's liberation in the period 1960–68?

Key points

- Success: 1964 Civil Rights Act
- Weakness: government refusal to enforce the sexual discrimination clause of the Civil Rights Act
- Success: NOW court cases
- Weakness: divisions within NOW
- Weakness: the failure to gain rights relating to sexuality and abortion

Introduction

The campaign for women's liberation saw successes and failures in the period 1960–68. The successes were the 1964 Civil Rights Act and NOW court cases. The weaknesses of the campaign were the government refusal to enforce the sexual discrimination clause of the Civil Rights Act, divisions within NOW, and the failure to gain rights related to sexuality and abortion.

Conclusion

The campaign for women's liberation saw successes and failures in the period 1960–68. Overall, the campaign was successful.

Hispanic Americans

Black Americans were not the only group to suffer racial discrimination in America. **Hispanic Americans**, particularly those of Mexican descent (**Chicanos**), suffered some of the most extreme poverty in America.

Chicano poverty

Many Chicano workers were employed in America's **agribusiness** as fruit pickers. In California, the average Chicano worker was employed for only 134 days a year. Therefore, the average income for Chicanos in California was only $1,378, far lower than the national average income of $7,850. Consequently, Chicano families made up 80 per cent of those claiming welfare in California.

César Chávez and his campaigns

César Chávez was the leading figure in the fight for Chicano rights. Like Martin Luther King, Chávez adopted non-violent means of protest.

In 1962, César Chávez established the National Farm Workers Association (NFWA), a **union** for Chicano workers. The union worked in three ways. First, it provided services, such as a **credit union**, for its members. Secondly, it negotiated with employers on behalf of its members. Finally, it provided legal advice for Chicano families in their dealings with local authorities.

La Huelga!, 1965

In 1965, the NFWA supported Filipino agricultural workers in launching *¡La Huelga!* – the strike. They demanded better wages for the 10,000 farm workers working in California's vineyards. In 1966, the NFWA merged with the Filipino Union, to form the United Farm Workers (UFW).

Peregrinacion, 1966

To support the strike, Chavez set out on a *peregrinación* (pilgrimage) covering 340 miles, from the vineyards of Delano to the offices of the Governor of California in Sacramento.

The Table Grape Boycott, 1968

Another way in which the UFW supported the strike was to launch the Table Grape Boycott in 1968. At its height, in 1970, 17 million Americans boycotted Californian grapes.

The achievements of UFW

- In 1970, the Delano grape producers were forced to raise the payment of workers to the national minimum wage.
- In 1975, the California Agricultural Labor Relations Act formally recognised the UFW's status as a union, forcing employers to negotiate with them.

Chicano blowouts, 1968

In 1966, a group of Chicano students, heavily influenced by the Black Panthers, established the Young Chicanos for Community Action (YCCA). YCCA became involved in the 'Chicano blowouts' of 1968. The blowouts were a series of protests in which thousands of Chicano students walked out of schools, demanding better standards of education for Hispanic students. The protests were successful in achieving bilingual education and a revised curriculum, including Chicano Studies.

Political gains

The Mexican American Political Association (MAPA) was created in 1960 in order to encourage Mexican Americans to register to vote. The proportion of Hispanic people registered to vote increased dramatically in the period 1960–72. In 1960, the proportion of Hispanic Americans registered to vote was less than five per cent. By 1972, it had risen to 44 per cent. In 1962, MAPA President, Edward Roybal, was elected to the **House of Representatives**.

Below are a series of definitions, a sample exam-style question and two sample conclusions. One of the conclusions achieves a high level because it contains an argument. The other achieves a lower level because it contains only description and assertion. Identify which is which. The mark scheme on page 3 will help you.

- **Description:** a detailed account.
- **Assertion:** a statement of fact or an opinion that is not supported by a reason.
- **Reason:** a statement that explains or justifies something.
- **Argument:** an assertion justified with a reason.

How far had the position of Hispanic Americans improved by 1968?

Sample 1

The position of Hispanic Americans was very bad at the beginning of the 1960s. For example, Chicanos employed in the fruit-picking business in California only made $1,378 per year (on average). They were seasonal workers and worked on average 134 days a year. César Chávez fought for Chicano rights with a number of protests. In 1965 he launched ¡La Huelga! (the strike). A year later, he embarked on a pilgrimage, and in 1968 he, and the UFW, launched the Table Grape Boycott. Also, the Chicano blowouts were launched to improve educational standards, and the Mexican American Political Association encouraged voter registration throughout the 1960s. All these things were done to try to improve the condition of Hispanic Americans in the years 1960–68.

Sample 2

The position of Hispanic Americans improved slightly in the period 1960–68 largely due to the efforts of César Chávez and the UFW. Chávez's three big campaigns ¡La Huelga!, Peregrinación, and the Table Grape Boycott brought about real change. Subsequent reforms allowed Chicano fruit pickers to earn the minimum wage and won official recognition for their unions. However, the reforms came after 1968. Nonetheless, there were political gains made within the period. The Chicano blowouts successfully forced a rise in educational standards, and the number of Mexican Americans registered to vote increased steadily during the 1960s.

Below are a sample exam-style question and a paragraph written in answer to this question. Read the paragraph and the mark scheme provided on page 3. Decide which level you would award the paragraph. Write the level below, along with a justification for your choice.

How far did the Civil Rights Act of 1964 end discrimination across America?

The Civil Rights Act of 1964 did not end discrimination in the American agribusiness. In California, many Mexican Americans (Chicanos) were discriminated against economically. In fact, 80 per cent of welfare cases in California came from Chicano families due to their poverty. Some attempts were made to address the problems of Chicano Americans living in California. César Chávez set up the National Farm Workers Union in 1962, which provided credit for its members and negotiated with employers on its members' behalf. However, any improvements this brought about had nothing to do with the Civil Rights Act.

Level: Reasons for choosing this level:

_____

_____

Native Americans

America's Native American community was also discriminated against. It faced extensive poverty and the threat that its tribal **reservations** would be abolished, forcing the community to lose its identity by integrating into mainstream society.

Issues facing Native Americans

Social and economic issues

In 1960, there were over 500,000 Native Americans living in America, of which about one-quarter lived on reservations. Life on the reservations was characterised by poverty. Unemployment on Native American reservations reached highs of 75 per cent during the 1960s. For example, among the 32,000 Native Americans on Navajo reservations, only 8,000 had a job with a regular wage in 1965. Poverty affected health, and the average life expectancy of Native Americans was only 44 years, 20 years fewer than the national average. Furthermore, unemployment led to social problems such as alcoholism. Indeed, 84 per cent of arrests made on Navajo reservations in 1960 were alcohol related.

Political issues

Native American reservations were managed by the Bureau of Indian Affairs (BIA). The Eisenhower Government wanted to solve the problems facing Native Americans through a policy of 'termination'. This policy proposed ending the special position of reservations and integrating Native Americans into mainstream society.

Campaigns

Campaigns against termination

The National Congress of American Indians (NCAI) opposed the policy of termination. Professor Sol Tax of the University of Chicago organised a conference in 1961 advocating the continuation of reservations, with greater power **devolved** to tribal leaders.

The National Indian Youth Council (NIYC), established in 1961, also campaigned against the policy of termination. In the late 1960s, NIYC, inspired by the Black Panthers, adopted 'Red Power', arguing for self-determination for Native Americans.

Alcatraz occupation

In 1964, a group of five Sioux Indians staged a short occupation of the island of Alcatraz. They wanted to turn the island into a cultural centre celebrating Native American history. The protestors offered to buy the island from the Government for the price at which it had been purchased from their ancestors. This amounted to 47 cents an acre, or a total of $9.40 for the island. The protest was unsuccessful, and after four hours, the protestors were removed by the police.

The achievements of Native American protest

In 1961, President Kennedy appointed Dr Philleo Nash as Head of the BIA. The BIA turned 56 reservations into 'redevelopment areas' that would receive government investment. President Johnson went further in the Indian Resources Development Act of 1967, allowing Native Americans to sell or mortgage their tribal land in order to raise money. Significantly, Professor Sol Tax's proposal that power be passed down to tribal leaders was highly influential at this time, and in 1966, the policy of compulsory termination was unofficially abandoned.

Below are a sample exam-style question and a timeline. Read the question, study the timeline and, using three coloured pens, put a red, amber or green star next to the events to show:

- red – events and policies that have no relevance to the question
- amber – events and policies that have some significance to the question
- green – events and policies that are directly relevant to the question.

1. How far had the position of Native Americans improved by 1968?

						Malcolm X assassinated	Freedom Cities movement begins	
						Selma campaign	César Chávez's *Peregrinación* (pilgrimage)	Memphis sanitation workers' strike
Greensboro sit-ins	Freedom Rides	National Farm Workers Association (NFWA) founded			President Johnson increases American involvement in Vietnam	March Against Fear	Chicano blowouts
Mexican American Political Association (MAPA) founded	National Indian Youth Council (NIYC) founded		Birmingham campaign	Sioux occupation of Alcatraz		Chicago campaign	Indian Resources Development Act	Poor People's campaign
1960	**1961**	**1962**	**1963**	**1964**	**1965**	**1966**	**1967**	**1968**
Civil Rights Act	Albany campaign begins	MAPA President, Edward Roybal, elected to the House of Representatives	March on Washington	Mississippi Freedom Summer	Publication of the Moynihan Report	NFWA merged with the Filipino Union to create the United Farm Workers (UFW)		*Commonwealth of Pennsylvania v. Daniel*
				Civil Rights Act	SDS organise anti-war marches in Washington D.C.	Black Panthers founded		CORE expels white members
					Voting Rights Act	The Diggers created an anarchist commune in San Francisco		Table Grape Boycott launched
					Launch of *¡La Huelga!*	SNCC expels white members		

Now repeat the activity with the following questions. You could use different colours, or number your stars 1, 2 and 3.

2. How far did the Civil Rights Act of 1964 end discrimination across America?

3. Why was protest culture so widespread in America in the period 1960–68?

Below is a list of suggested further reading on this topic.

- Peter Braunstein and Michael William Doyle, *Imagine Nation: The American Counterculture of the 1960s and 1970s* (Routledge, 2002), pages 159–188.
- Vivienne Sanders, *Civil Rights in the USA 1945–1968* (Hodder Education, 2008), pages 156–162.
- Randy Shaw, *Beyond the Fields: César Chávez and the UFW* (University of California Press, 2008), pages 13–50.

Exam focus

Below is a sample A-grade essay. Read the essay and the examiner's comments around it.

Why was protest culture so widespread in the period 1960–68?

The introduction sets out a range of factors to be discussed, including the campaigns of black people, as well as setting up the argument that will continue throughout the whole essay.

Protest culture was very widespread in America in the period 1960–68 due to the widespread discrimination facing American citizens during these years and because of the effectiveness of protest as a method for addressing inequality. Discrimination affected black people, Native Americans, Chicanos and women. In addition, many students joined the protest culture because they wanted to challenge the values of mainstream culture and America's involvement in the Vietnam War. All of these groups used protest to challenge discrimination and try to make America a fairer country.

This paragraph covers the entire period specified in the question, as well as discussing the civil rights movement and the Black Power movement. The examples are brief, but show a thorough understanding of the nature of their campaigns.

Black people protested in order to challenge racial discrimination. In the South, the central issues were segregation and disenfranchisement. Campaigns such as the sit-ins of 1960, the Freedom Rides of 1961, the Birmingham campaign of 1963 and the March on Washington of the same year tackled segregation, whereas the Mississippi Freedom Summer and the Selma campaign focused on voting rights. In the North, campaigns such as the Black Panthers' 'Patrol the Pigs' campaign took on police brutality, while SNCC's Freedom Cities and the Panthers' Freedom Schools addressed inadequate educational provision. Protest was widespread in the black community because of the desire within the community to address racial discrimination, whether it was segregation in the South or police brutality in the North.

This paragraph links Red Power to Black Power, arguing that black radicals inspired protest in other communities. In so doing, it answers the question and links different aspects of the essay.

Native Americans faced important political problems, which centred on the policy of termination. This was the Government's policy of ending the reservation system and forcing Native Americans to integrate into mainstream society. In response to the political problems, in 1961 the National Congress of American Indians held a conference that advocated passing power from the Bureau of Indian Affairs to tribal chiefs. More radical were the National Indian Youth Council who occupied the island of Alcatraz in 1964 in order to draw attention to the exploitation of Native Americans and the attacks on their culture. Later, inspired by the Black Panthers, this group adopted the slogan 'Red Power' and called for self-determination for Native Americans. Protest culture spread to the Native American community because of the desire within that community to resist the policy of termination. In addition, Native American protest was inspired by the slogans and demands of the Black Power movement.

The essay uses precise details to exemplify the poverty experienced by Chicano families.

The problems facing Chicanos also led to protest. In California, Chicanos were employed in the agribusiness as seasonal fruit pickers. As a result, Chicano workers were only employed for 134 days a year, and earned, on average, $1,378 a year, compared to the average annual salary of $7,850 for Americans more generally. Due to these problems César Chávez, leader of the United Farm Workers, a union representing Chicano and Filipino workers, mounted a series of protests to get better wages for his members. These included ¡La Huelga!, a strike that affected the Delano vineyards; the Peregrinación, a personal pilgrimage from the vineyards of Delano to Sacramento, the capital of California; and a boycott of table grapes. In this way, the protest culture spread to Chicano and Filipino workers because it was necessary to address the poverty that plagued their lives.

Women also protested against sexual discrimination. Second wave feminists, many of who were members of the National Organisation for Women (NOW), protested against sexual discrimination in the workplace. NOW's legal team used the terms of the Civil Rights Act (1964) to take the telecoms company Southern Bell to court and force them to promote Lorena Weeks who had been refused a promotion because she was a woman. Third wave feminists, some of who left NOW in order to fight for the rights of lesbians, campaigned for women's rights in a different sense. New York Radical Women held 'Speak Outs', events at which women could share their feelings about having an abortion. They also held an alternative Miss America pageant at which they crowned a sheep as Miss America. This was a protest against the conventional view of what made women beautiful. Again, women engaged in protest because of the huge problems they faced — problems at work, problems to do with the availability of abortion, and problems concerning sexual stereotypes.

Students also became involved in protest. In the early 1960s, university students founded Students for a Democratic Society (SDS). SDS objected to the consumer culture and the corporate culture that dominated America in the 1960s. They argued that a truly democratic society was only possible if there was economic equality. By the mid-1960s, students were protesting against the Vietnam War. The central issue was the draft, which forced young men to join up and fight for their country in East Asia. SDS organised a series of anti-war marches in Washington D.C. In April 1965, 20,000 people marched for peace, and 20,000 more joined the SDS march in November. Students joined the protest culture partly to protest about the mass culture that was developing in the 1960s, but mostly to put pressure on the Government to end its war in Vietnam.

In conclusion, protest culture was widespread for the simple reason that there was a lot to protest about. Black people in the South campaigned against segregation and disenfranchisement while their brothers and sisters in the North protested against police brutality. For Native Americans, termination was the main issue, whilst Chicanos and Filipinos campaigned for an end to their poverty. Second wave feminists campaigned against sexual discrimination at work, while third wave feminists campaigned against sexual stereotypes. Finally, students campaigned against the draft and the war in Vietnam. In short, America was a society in which many people were unhappy. In this context, the successes of the black civil rights movement offered hope to those who employed protest to challenge discrimination.

Here, the candidate distinguishes between two different waves of feminism. The distinction is accurate and extends the scope of the essay.

This paragraph further extends the range of the essay, discussing student protest before and after the Vietnam War.

The conclusion supports the main argument of the essay by pointing to the various grievances that led to protest during the 1960s. In addition, brief reference is made to the influence of the civil rights movement on subsequent protest movements.

26/30

This essay considers a wide range of protests, drawing on the civil rights movement and Black Power as well as material from the fourth part of the specification. The essay makes the argument that protest was widespread because there was a lot to protest about. In addition, the impact of the black civil rights movement is alluded to. The essay is awarded a mark in Level 5 because of the sustained focus on the question and the range and depth of material used. However, the simplicity of the argument keeps it low within the level.

What makes a good answer?

You have now considered four sample A-grade essays (see pages 14, 34, 46 and above). Use these essays to make a bullet-pointed list of the characteristics of an A-grade essay. Use this list when planning and writing your own practice exam essays.

Timeline

1868
Fourteenth Amendment – gave equal citizenship rights to everyone born in America

1870
Fifteenth Amendment – gave voting rights to all citizens regardless of race

1890s
Southern states begin to introduce Jim Crow laws

1896
Plessy v. Ferguson

1944
Smith v. Allwright

1946
Morgan v. Virginia

1947
Journey of Reconciliation
Publication of 'To Secure These Rights'
NAACP picketed department stores in New Orleans
End of the CNO voter registration campaign in Arkansas

1948
Executive order 9980 outlawed racial discrimination in the civil service
Executive order 9981 ended segregation in the army

1949
Truman's inauguration ceremony is desegregated

1950
Sweatt v. Painter
Canteen at Washington Airport is desegregated

1951
NAACP school boycotts
Committee on Government Contract Compliance established

1953
UDL bus boycott in Louisiana
Earl Warren appointed to the Supreme Court

1954
Brown v. Board of Education

1955
Brown II
Lynching of Emmett Till
Beginning of the Montgomery Bus Boycott

1956
Browder v. Gayle
End of the Montgomery Bus Boycott

1957
Southern Christian Leadership Conference (SCLC) created
Civil Rights Act
Little Rock campaign

1958
Cooper v. Aaron

1960
Greensboro sit-ins

Student Non-violent Co-ordinating Committee (SNCC) founded
Mexican American Political Association (MAPA) founded
Civil Rights Act
Boynton v. Virginia

1961
Freedom Rides
National Indian Youth Council (NIYC) founded
Albany campaign begins

1962
National Farm Workers Association (NFWA) founded
MAPA President, Edward Roybal, elected to the House of
    Representatives

1963
Birmingham campaign
March on Washington

1964
Sioux occupation of Alcatraz
Malcolm X leaves the Nation of Islam and forms the Organisation of
    Afro-American Unity (OAAU)
Mississippi Freedom Summer
Civil Rights Act

1965
Malcolm X assassinated
Selma campaign
President Johnson increases American involvement in Vietnam
Publication of the Moynihan Report
Elementary and Secondary Education Act
SDS organise anti-war marches in Washington D.C.
Voting Rights Act
Launch of *¡La Huelga!*
Higher Education Act

1966
Freedom Cities movement begins
César Chávez's *Peregrinación* (pilgrimage)
March Against Fear
Chicago campaign
NFWA merged with the Filipino Union to create the United Farm
    Workers (UFW)
Black Panthers founded
The Diggers create an anarchist commune in San Francisco
SNCC expelled white members

1967
Indian Resources Development Act

1968
Memphis sanitation workers' strike
Chicano blowouts
Martin Luther King assassinated
Civil Rights Act
Poor People's campaign
Commonwealth of Pennsylvania v. Daniel
CORE expelled white members
Table Grape Boycott launched

1969
Weeks v. Southern Bell

Glossary

Agribusiness The term for the farming business. It includes the growing, harvesting, processing and packing of farmed produce.

Allah God's name in Islam.

American Civil War A military conflict from 1861–1865 between the Southern states and the Northern states. The Southern states withdrew from the United States in order to protect their way of life, which included slavery, from the more industrial and urban Northern states. The War led to the abolition of slavery across the United States.

Angela Davis Professor of Philosophy at University of California, Los Angeles. Davis was a well-known black activist who worked with SNCC and the Black Panthers.

Betty Friedan Author of *The Feminine Mystique* (1963), Friedan argued that women needed to seize their independence through paid employment and education. She was a founding member of NOW.

Bill A proposed law. It becomes an Act once it is formally recognised as a law.

Bill of Rights The first ten **Constitutional Amendments**. They guarantee rights such as freedom of speech and assembly.

Black Nationalism A political philosophy and movement that stresses the need for black people to work together to achieve their economic and political independence. It also often focuses on the achievements and importance of African culture and history.

Black Power A political philosophy and movement that focuses on racial integration from a position of strength. Black Power groups tend to argue that black people should spearhead the fight for racial justice, and only work with white people or white groups on their own terms.

Black Power salute A political gesture, which involves punching the air with a clenched fist.

Black separatism The idea that black people can only be free if they live in an exclusively black community.

Capitalism An economic system based on the private ownership of property, in which goods and services are distributed according to the market.

Chicanos A term used to describe Americans of Mexican descent. The term became widely used during the struggle for Chicano rights in the 1960s and 1970s.

Citizen A person who is recognised as being part of a specific national community, such as the USA. Citizens have legal rights, as well as responsibilities such as the duty to pay tax.

Civil rights groups A collective term for groups that were fighting for greater political rights for black Americans such as the NAACP, SNCC, SCLC and CORE.

Civil rights movement A term used to describe the collection of civil rights groups who fought for racial justice. The civil rights movement was not united under a single leadership.

Civil service People employed by the Government. They are often tasked with implementing Government policy.

CNO Committee on Negro Organisation – an early civil rights group that pioneered peaceful protest.

Cold War A period of heightened political tension between the capitalist West, led by America, and the communist East, led by the Soviet Union.

Communal self-defence The idea that people have the right to defend their community when it is attacked.

Communists Members of the Communist Party. The FBI were concerned that communists were loyal to the Soviet Union rather than America and that they were working to overthrow the American Government.

Community self-help A situation in which the needs of a community are looked after by the community, rather than relying on outside help.

Congress The American Parliament, consisting of two houses, the Senate and the House of Representatives.

Congressmen Members of the American Parliament.

Constitution The fundamental laws that govern a country and specify the rights and duties of citizens and the Government. The American Constitution is a written document that came into force in 1787.

Constitutional Amendments Changes to the American Constitution.

CORE The Congress of Racial Equality – a civil rights group founded in 1942.

Court case A dispute between individuals or groups that is taken to a court of law in order to be resolved.

Credit union A group that is controlled by its members and provides cheap loans to its members.

Democratic Controlled by the people.

Democratic Party One of the two main political parties in modern America. Traditionally, the Democrats supported slavery and then, in the South, segregation. Since the Second World War, they have become associated with advancing black rights.

Democratisation The process of making something more democratic.

Devolve To transfer power from a central organisation to a local one.

Disenfranchised Denied the right to vote.

Dixiecrats A group of Southern members of the Democratic Party who were committed to maintaining racial segregation.

Double V A campaign, and a hand gesture, indicating that soldiers were fighting for a double victory: a victory against racism in Europe and in America.

Draft cards Official cards sent by the American Government to young men, informing them that they were eligible to be called up to fight in the Vietnam War.

Elijah Muhammad The leader of the Nation of Islam from 1934 until his death in 1975.

Elvis Presley An influential rock 'n' roll singer, sometimes described as the King of Rock 'n' Roll.

Emancipation The act of setting someone free.

Executive order An order issued by the American president, changing the way in which the Government works.

Fair Deal A programme of welfare and housing reform introduced by President Johnson.

FBI Federal Bureau of Investigation – the federal police force.

Federal Government The national government of America.

Filibuster A method used in the Senate to prevent the passage of a law. There is only a limited amount of time to consider a bill. Members of the Senate can take advantage of this by filibustering: prolonging debate of a bill to use up time and prevent or delay members voting the bill into law.

Gandhi Mohandas Gandhi – an Indian political leader who played a crucial role in the struggle for Indian independence.

Ghetto A deprived area of a city.

GIs A slang term for American soldiers.

Grandfather clause A law that disqualified black people from voting. Following the Fifteenth Amendment of 1870, it was illegal to disqualify people from voting due to their race. The grandfather clause disqualified people whose grandfathers could not vote. In this sense, they **disenfranchised** black people without breaking the Fifteenth Amendment.

Grass roots A slang term usually applied to political movements that are rooted in the community.

Great Depression A period of extreme economic recession, which lasted from 1929 to around 1945.

Hispanic Americans Americans originating from Spanish-speaking countries in Central and South America.

House of Representatives One of the two houses of Congress (the American Parliament).

Inauguration A formal ceremony marking the beginning of a president's term in office.

Individualistic Prioritising the needs, wants and values of the individual over those of the community.

Interstate A term that describes any kind of service, business or government agency which functions across more than one state.

J. Edgar Hoover The first head of the Federal Bureau of Investigation (FBI). Hoover played a key role in founding the FBI. He is credited with introducing modern methods of police work to the FBI, but was also criticised for the method that he encouraged COINTELPRO (Counter Intelligence Program) to combat communism.

James Dean A film star, who became famous for playing misunderstood young rebels.

James Meredith In 1962, he became the first black student to attend the University of Mississippi.

Jesus The central figure in the Christian religion.

Jim Crow laws Local laws that were used across the South to legally segregate public places and facilities.

KKK The Ku Klux Klan; a white supremacist group, largely based in the South. It terrorised those who campaigned against racism. Often members of the KKK were also members of the police force or local government and therefore it was difficult for the authorities to bring them to justice.

Kwame Nkrumah The first leader of independent Ghana. He had been a leader in the fight to liberate Ghana from the British Empire.

Letter from Birmingham Jail A letter written by Martin Luther King during his time in jail in Birmingham. He used the letter to defend his methods against his critics who thought that he was being too provocative.

Literacy tests Tests used in some Southern states that disqualified black people from voting on the grounds that they were not sufficiently good at reading and writing to be allowed to vote.

Lynching A type of killing in which a mob of people hang a person, usually from a tree.

Miles Davis A jazz musician and composer.

Moynihan Report A report published in 1965 officially titled *The Negro Family: The Case for National Action*. The report was written by the sociologist Daniel Patrick Moynihan. It was controversial as some black radicals argued that it blamed black people for their own poverty.

NAACP The National Association for the Advancement of Colored People – one of America's oldest civil rights groups. By the 1960s it was best known for its legal campaigns.

National Guard A part-time military force, used to keep the peace in the case of emergencies.

Nazi Belonging, or to do with, the Nazi Party – the ruling political party in Germany under Hitler.

Northern states States in which there was little or no formal racial segregation. Generally speaking, the Northern states had abolished slavery before the Southern states and as a result there was much less legal discrimination against black Americans. Northern states also tended to be more industrial and urban than Southern states.

OAAU The Organization of Afro-American Unity – a black rights group founded by Malcolm X in 1964.

Peaceful protest A form of protest in which people use non-violent means such as marches, boycotts and sit-ins to try to bring about change.

Picket A form of peaceful protest in which people stand outside a building to draw attention to their campaign.

Pimp A person who makes money by managing prostitutes.

Pistol-whipping A type of beating in which one person hits another repeatedly with a gun.

Political idealism A quality of some activists or political campaigners who focus on wanting to radically change the world for the better.

Primary elections The first round of an election, used to select the candidates for a subsequent election.

Racial segregation A situation in which people of different races are forced, either by law or circumstance, to live separately and use separate facilities.

Radical A person who seeks fundamental social change.

Republican Party One of America's two main political parties. During the nineteenth century, the Republicans were associated with the industrial and urban North, and with efforts to abolish slavery. Since the Second World War, the Republicans have been associated with the defence of the free market, and criticisms of the welfare state.

Reservations Land that is set aside for the use of Native Americans.

Rosa Parks A member of the NAACP who is remembered for refusing to give up her bus seat to a white man and therefore sparking the Montgomery Bus Boycott.

School board A local government body that supervises the provision of education in a particular area of America.

SCLC The Southern Christian Leadership Conference – a civil rights group formed after the Montgomery Bus Boycott. In contrast to the NAACP, it did not accept individual members. Instead, it comprise a committee of people who helped to organise civil rights protests across America.

Second wave feminism Feminism that focused on social and economic equality between men and women. In contrast, first wave feminism fought for female voting rights.

Senate The upper house of the American Parliament.

Sickle cell anaemia A blood disease that mainly affects black people.

Sit-in A form of peaceful protest, which involves sitting in an area and refusing to leave.

Slave A person who is legally considered the property of another person. A slave has no rights and can be treated in any way his or her master sees fit.

SNCC The Student Non-violent Co-ordinating Committee – a civil rights group that was formed by students after the success of the sit-in movement.

Southern states A group of states in the south-east of America. The word South is used to describe a particular culture rather than a geographical area. From the 1890s, the South was characterised by segregation.

Soviet Union A group of communist countries dominated by the Soviet Union, one of the two superpowers during the Cold War.

Supreme Court America's highest court of law.

Swahili An African language.

Teach-ins A form of protest in which students and teachers take over a university. Teach-ins are different to regular lectures as they usually focus on radical subjects.

Third wave feminism A form of feminism which focuses on the private, personal and psychological causes of women's inequality. Third wave feminists tend to argue that 'the personal is the political' and therefore are critical of relationships such as marriage, and activities such as heterosexual sex, which they think has traditionally led to female enslavement. Many third wave feminists in the late 1960s advocated female separatism, in other words, living in an all female community, or lesbianism as essential aspects of women's liberation.

UDL The United Defence League – a civil rights group formed in 1953.

Uncle Tom A slang term for a black person who is extremely willing to serve white people. The term refers to the character from the Harriet Beecher Stowe's book *Uncle Tom's Cabin* (1852).

Underclass A group of people who are unable to find regular work and therefore are forced to live in poverty and often turn to crime.

Union An organisation of workers that fights for the rights of its members.

United Nations An international organisation set up in 1945. The UN promotes co-operation between the countries of the world, with the aim of ensuring world peace.

Vietnam War A conflict that took place in East Asia from 1955 until 1975. American troops were sent to fight in Vietnam in large numbers from 1964, although America had been involved in the War since the 1950s. The American Government believed that it needed to send troops in order to stop the spread of communism in Asia.

Voter registration campaigns A campaign to encourage people to register to vote.

White supremacists People who believe that white people are naturally superior to other races and therefore have the right to dominate other races.

William S. Burroughs An experimental American writer. His novels, which describe his experiences on heroin, influenced the Beatniks.

Woodrow Crockett One of the Tuskegee Airmen, the first group of black fighter pilots to be trained by the American air force. The Tuskegee Airmen flew 200 missions during the Second World War and never lost a single plane.

Answers

Section 1: The social and economic position of black citizens in the USA, 1945–55

Page 5, Complete the paragraph: suggested answer

The Second World War was an important reason for the advancement in black civil rights in the period 1945–55. For example, the Second World War led to mass migration of black workers from the Southern states to the North. Around half a million black Americans made this journey and received higher wages in Northern industry as a result. Equally, the Second World War highlighted the evil of racism in Europe. Black soldiers who fought against Nazi racism started making the Double V sign to show that they were fighting against racism at home as well as abroad. Finally, black airmen, such as Woodrow Crockett, were regarded as heroes by white officers and white soldiers. **In this way, the Second World War advanced black civil rights because it changed the status of black Americans as well as improving the economic prospects of those who moved North to find work.**

Page 5, Identify an argument

Paragraph 2 contains the argument.

Page 7, Spot the mistake

The paragraph does not get into Level 4 because, although it is accurate, focused and contains a clear link back to the question, the examples it contains are highly generalised.

Page 7, Turning assertion into argument: suggested answer

President Truman's attempts to desegregate public places did little to tackle racial inequality in the sense that **his three acts of desegregation affected either very specific or very limited aspects of American life.**

'To Secure These Rights' had a limited impact on racial inequality in the sense that **although it highlighted the problems correctly, many of its recommendations were not implemented.**

President Truman's employment reforms had a moderate impact on racial inequality in the sense that **they outlawed discrimination in government jobs alone.**

Page 11, Develop the detail: suggested answer

The Brown case was a very significant achievement in the campaign for racial equality in the period 1945–55. For example, the case overturned ***Plessy v. Ferguson***, the ruling that had justified segregation for many years **and legalised the Jim Crow laws in the Southern states**. It also showed that the court was sympathetic to the campaign. **In fact, the court went as far as to end the doctrine of 'separate but equal'.** However, white people reacted badly to the ruling. **For example, White Citizens Councils were created to resist integration, and by 1956 these had 250,000 members. In addition, the KKK lynched Emmett Till in 1955. Furthermore, 101 Southern Congressmen signed The Southern Manifesto calling for resistance to desegregation.** Also, the change in the law did not lead to a change in reality **as, by 1957, only three per cent of black students in the Southern states were in integrated schools**. Despite this, the Brown case was very significant because it overturned the legal basis for segregation.

Section 2: Martin Luther King and peaceful protest, 1955–68

Page 17, Eliminate irrelevance

In the area of education, some progress had been made towards racial equality by 1955. In 1954, the NAACP took the Brown case to the Supreme Court. ~~The NAACP used court cases to campaign for greater rights for black Americans. The Supreme Court was America's highest court of law. People took cases to the Supreme Court when they believed that their rights, as set out in the American Constitution, had been violated.~~ The NAACP's Brown case resulted in the ruling that segregation in education was illegal. This overturned the ruling of *Plessy v. Ferguson,* ~~which had been the result of a case brought to the Supreme Court by a man called Homer Plessy~~. Despite the significance of the Brown ruling, the case failed to create widespread change. Indeed, even following Brown II – which ruled that change should occur 'with all deliberate speed' – and the Little Rock campaign, which sought to speed up school desegregation, change was slow to occur. By 1957, 97 per cent of black students in the Southern states remained in segregated schools. ~~This problem continued throughout the 1960s, and is one reason why racial equality had not been achieved by 1968.~~

Page 19, Complete the paragraph: suggested answer

The civil rights movement achieved a great deal because of its policy of non-violent direct action. For example, **the Greensboro sit-ins of 1960 rapidly grew in size, and by the end of 1961 sit-ins and similar activities had forced the desegregation of public places in 810 towns across the South. Equally, the Freedom Rides turned the** *de jure* **victories of** *Morgan v. Virginia* **and** *Boynton v. Virginia* **into** *de facto* **change. What is more, the Freedom Rides were successful because media coverage of the violence of white racists horrified America and forced President Kennedy to intervene and order the desegregation of interstate buses and interstate bus facilities.** Clearly, non-violent direct action was a very effective tool in advancing civil rights because it gained media attention and the sympathy of white opinion in the North.

Page 19, Identify an argument

Paragraph 1 contains the argument.

Page 21, Spot the mistake

The paragraph does not get into Level 4 because, although it presents an accurate and detailed narrative of relevant events, it does not provide an explicit link back to the question. Therefore, it attempts analysis rather than analysing fully.

Page 21, Eliminate irrelevance

King was not the only important factor; other civil rights groups also played an important role. ~~CORE was founded in 1941 and its support grew during the war as black pride and status improved. In 1947, CORE ran the Journey of Reconciliation to test the ruling *Morgan v. Virginia.*~~ In 1961, CORE took to the buses again in the Freedom Rides, this time testing the 1960 ruling *Boynton v. Virginia*. CORE played a significant role in this regard, as the protest showed that *de jure* change had not led to *de facto* change. What is more, the Freedom Rides forced President Kennedy to oversee the desegregation of interstate transport and transport facilities, another important victory for the movement. ~~Kennedy became president in 1961, but only governed until his assassination in 1963.~~ The NAACP was also important in forcing *de jure* change. For example, they were involved in the court cases ~~*Sweatt v. Painter*~~, *Browder v. Gayle*, *Cooper v. Aaron* and *Boynton v. Virginia*. These court cases further undermined the legality of segregation. In this way, CORE and the NAACP played an important role in the campaign for racial equality because, through legal challenges and non-violent protest, they rolled back segregation in the South.

Page 25, Develop the detail: suggested answer

In the area of voting, significant progress had been made by 1965. For example, even though Eisenhower's Civil Rights Act did not add many voters to the electoral roll **(in total, the 1957 and 1960 Acts added only three per cent more black voters to the electoral roll)**, the 1965 Act was much more successful. The Act had many provisions that were much more effective than previous Acts. **For example, it outlawed all tests, such as literacy tests, and clauses, such as grandfather clauses, which prevented black citizens from voting. In addition, it gave the Government the power to enforce the provisions of the Act.** As a result, many more black people registered to vote in the years following 1965. **Indeed, by 1966, 230,000 more black people had registered to vote across the South.** There were also limitations to the success of the Act. In fact, in the year after the Act, there were still a number of states where a minority of black citizens were able to vote. **In fact, four Southern states still had fewer than 50 per cent of their black citizens registered to vote.** In this way, *de jure* racial equality had been achieved, but *de facto* equality was slower to follow.

Page 27, Turning assertion into argument: suggested answer

Martin Luther King's campaigns in the North were hampered by a lack of support from Northern whites because **social and economic change would have to be funded by increased taxes and they were unwilling to contribute in this way.**

President Johnson was less sympathetic to King's later campaigns because **King had publically criticised Johnson's policy of war in Vietnam, and because Johnson's financial priority was the Vietnam War not civil rights.**

Martin Luther King had less support in Chicago's black community because **church attendance was lower in the Northern states and so fewer black people were inspired by King's Christian message.**

Page 29, Develop the detail: suggested answer

Political opposition slowed down progress towards racial equality significantly prior to 1964.

For example, early civil rights bills, **such as Eisenhower's Acts of 1957 and 1960**, were weakened by Congress. Congress had a variety of methods for weakening bills. **For example, in 1957, Congress watered down the Civil Rights Act by reducing the penalty for denying black citizens their right to vote to a mere $1,000 fine or six months in prison. In addition, Congressmen could filibuster in order to slow the passage of bills. Indeed, in 1964, Senators filibustered – unsuccessfully – for 83 days.** The presidents also played a role in slowing progress. One president, **Eisenhower**, was initially unwilling to use his power to force the pace of change. **He was reluctant to intervene at Little Rock because he believed that black people should wait until the time was right for integration.** Even Johnson was less helpful towards the end of the 1960s **as he was distracted by the Vietnam War.** Nonetheless, between 1964 and 1965, political opposition could not prevent the passing of two major Acts to promote racial equality **– the Civil Rights Act of 1964, and the Voting Rights Act of 1965**. In this way, opposition did slow down progress towards racial equality, but was unable to prevent it.

Page 31, You're the examiner

The paragraph should be awarded Level 4 because it includes a wide range of accurate detail that is relevant to the question. In addition, it shows clear focus on the question and the final sentence analyses the role played by King.

Section 3: Black Power and the use of violence

Page 37, Complete the paragraph: suggested answer

One reason why black protest became more radical during the 1960s was the influence of Malcolm X. Malcolm X put forward a series of very convincing criticisms of Martin Luther King. First, he argued that Martin Luther King was an 'Uncle Tom', by which he meant he slavishly obeyed his white masters. Secondly, he criticised Martin Luther King's pacifism, arguing that it was natural to want to defend yourself and your community. Finally, he argued that Martin Luther King's dream was in fact a nightmare, as integration would lead to a new kind of slavery for black people. **In this way, black protest became more radical during the 1960s because of Malcolm X's powerful criticisms of the traditional civil rights movement.**

Page 37, Eliminate irrelevance

One of the reasons why the civil rights movement was increasingly divided during the 1960s was the influence of Malcolm X and the Nation of Islam. ~~Malcolm X had a tragic early life due to the murder of his father and his mother's nervous breakdown.~~ He argued in favour of 'Black Nationalism'. By this he meant that black people should govern themselves rather than being controlled by white politicians and that black people should be self-sufficient through community control of the economies within the ghettos. This message was extremely popular amongst the black working class in the Northern states because, unlike Martin Luther King's message, it addressed the social and economic problems of the Northern ghettos. ~~Also, the Nation of Islam taught that white people were created by a white scientist named Yacub.~~ In this way, the civil rights movement became increasingly divided because Malcolm X offered an attractive alternative to the campaign for integration.

Page 39, Identify an argument

Paragraph 1 contains the argument.

Page 39, Turning assertion into argument: suggested answer

The shooting of James Meredith contributed to the emergence of Black Power because **it persuaded many black radicals of the need for self-defence.**

The influence of Malcolm X was a key reason for the emergence of Black Power because **many black radicals were persuaded by his criticisms of the civil rights movement.**

Criticisms of Martin Luther King led to the emergence of Black Power because **they exposed the limitations of peaceful protest and made more radical alternatives more attractive.**

Page 41, You're the examiner

The paragraph should be awarded Level 2 because, although there is some accurate and relevant detail, the paragraph does not focus on the question and the range and depth of supporting material is very limited.

Section 4: The changing economic and social environment of the 1960s

Page 49, Eliminate irrelevance

In lots of ways American society was not dominated by the cult of individual freedom. At work, more and more people were working for big businesses with a corporate culture that demanded conformity. In big corporations, the emphasis was on impressing your boss rather than standing out as an individual. ~~Corporations produced a great deal of money which financed impressive projects that formed part of Kennedy's 'New Frontier'. The most impressive was the space program, which Kennedy had committed to landing a man on the moon.~~ Equally, leisure time was dominated by the mass media, particularly television programmes. In fact, by 1960, 90 per cent of Americans lived in a household with a television. ~~Martin Luther King and other civil rights leaders used this new medium to get their message about black rights across to the whole of America.~~ The consumer boom of the 1960s also meant that more and more people were buying the same kinds of products. In this way, there were large aspects of American life where individualism seemed to be under attack.

Page 51, Develop the detail: suggested answer

Counterculture in the 1960s was very successful. For example, the student movement grew in popularity after the outbreak of the Vietnam War, staging a number of protests. **Membership of SDS increased from 1,500 in 1965 to 30,000 by 1967. SDS staged two large anti-war protests in 1965: in April, 20,000 people marched in Washington D.C., and in November, 40,000 people marched against the War.** In addition, the hippie movement was very popular amongst young people and a number of notable communes were formed. **For example, in 1966, The Diggers established a commune in San Francisco, which provided free healthcare and free drugs for its members.** The drug culture also played a significant role in the success of the movement, **particularly amongst hippies and beatniks**. Writers and artists formed part of this movement, publishing works that challenged accepted traditions, **such as William S. Burroughs' book *Naked Lunch* (1959)**. In this way, the counterculture movement of the 1960s succeeded in gaining the support of many young people, spreading its anti-war message and its countercultural values through literature and drugs.

Page 55, Identify an argument

Paragraph 2 contains the argument.

Page 55, You're the examiner

The paragraph should be awarded Level 3 because it is focused on the question, it contains some accurate supporting material, and it attempts analysis.

Notes